"Mark Dever has rendered an invaluable service to the Body of Christ in this book. Its biblical grounding is sure, and its theological insights are *spot on!* Few address the issues of ecclesiology better than this pastor/theologian. This work will help us better understand what the church is and what the church does when it is faithful to Scripture."

Daniel L. Akin
President, Southeastern Baptist Theological Seminary

"Mark Dever has taught me more about the church than any other living human being. He's a keen observer and insightful practitioner. In *The Church: The Gospel Made Visible*, Dever helps us to see how the good news goes cinematic in the nitty-gritty lives of local congregations. What joy comes from recognizing the embodiment of the gospel in our very ordinary congregations!"

Thabiti Anyabwile
Senior pastor, First Baptist Church, Grand Cayman Islands

"The church today desperately needs to think more deeply about the church. That's why I'm incredibly thankful for Mark Dever. No one writes as passionately, as winsomely, as biblically, or as practically about the church. This book is a wonderful example of all those traits. Even though my theology is different on a few important points like baptism and congregationalism, I always learn from Mark when he talks ecclesiology. If you love the church, you'll love this book. And if the doctrine of the church sounds terribly unimportant, then you need to read this book even more."

Kevin DeYoung
Senior pastor, University Reformed Church, East Lansing, Michigan

"I'm not sure that I know anyone who has read more on ecclesiology, from the whole breadth of the Christian tradition, than Mark Dever. So, his exegesis is not done in isolation but in conversation with twenty centuries of Christian thinking. As a Presbyterian, I would encourage non-Baptists and non-congregationalists to read and engage with Mark's work, not only because it is so well done, biblical, and helpful, but also because of a huge evangelical blind spot the book addresses. Ecclesiology is indisputably one of evangelicalism's great weaknesses, in part because of subjectivism, individualism, and pragmatism. Mark offers a robust corrective to this, and even where you may disagree you will find yourself edified and instructed. Mark approaches this subject not simply as a skilled historical theologian and systematician, but also as a local church pastor who has fostered a vital and healthy embrace of biblical polity in his own congregation, with happy results. He is no "dry-land sailor" or impractical theoretician but a faithful shepherd. The growth and life and fruitfulness of his flock testify to this."

Ligon Duncan
Senior minister, First Presbyterian Church, Jackson, Mississippi

"Trust me, if you talk with my friend Mark Dever for more than five minutes, the local church will come up in the conversation—not only because it is the focus of his impressive academic work, but because the church is to him as it was to Charles Spurgeon, 'the dearest place on earth.' Over many discussions Mark has taught me much about the church, and even in areas where we disagree, I've been affected by his passion for the church. This book allows you to have a similar conversation with Mark, and I have no doubt that your heart will be stirred with love for the church universal and for your local church in particular."

C. J. Mahaney
President, Sovereign Grace Ministries

"For far too long, the church has suffered for its lack of attention to ecclesiology. Thankfully, that neglect has given way to a new age of rediscovery, and Mark Dever has been a key catalyst for the recovery of biblical ecclesiology. In this book, you will find a faithful, truthful, thrilling understanding of the church. But be warned: Once you read this book, you will never be satisfied until you are a part of a church that is growing into this kind of faithfulness and life."

R. Albert Mohler, Jr.
President, The Southern Baptist Theological Seminary

IX 9Marks

The Church

The
Gospel
Made
Visible

Mark Dever

ACADEMIC
Nashville, Tennessee

Published by B&H Publishing Group
Nashville, Tennessee

Dewey Decimal Classification: 262.7
Subject Heading: CHURCH GOVERNMENT AND POLITY \ CHURCH \
CHURCH MEMBERSHIP

Printed in the United States of America

2 3 4 5 6 7 8 9 10 11 12 • 17 16 15 14 13 12

Dedication

To Mike McKinley,
Greg Gilbert,
Michael Lawrence,
Aaron Menikoff,
Andy Davis,
David Platt,
Matt Chandler,
J. D. Greear,

and the rising generation of pastors called
to shepherd "the flock of God" (1 Pet 5:2).

Contents

Preface: The Need for Studying the Doctrine of the Church

F or too many Christians today, the doctrine of the church is like a decoration on the front of a building. Maybe it's pretty, maybe it's not, but finally it's unimportant because it bears no weight.

Yet nothing could be further from the truth. The doctrine of the church is of the utmost importance. It is the most visible part of Christian theology, and it is vitally connected with every other part.[1] "Christ's work is the church's foundation. . . . Christ's work continues in the church; the

---

[1] John Webster considered how God's people are central to God's creation: "Out of the plentitude and limitless perfection of his own self-originating life as Father, Son and Spirit, God determines to be God with his creatures. This directedness of God to creatures has its eternal origin in the purpose of the Father. The Father wills that *ex nihilo* there should come into being a creaturely counterpart to the fellowship of love which is the inner life of the Holy Trinity. This purpose is put into effect by God the Son, who is both maker and remaker of creatures, calling them into being and calling them back into being when they have fallen into estrangement from the one through whom and for whom they are made. And the divine purpose is perfected in the Spirit. The Spirit completes creatures by sustaining them in life, directing their course so that they attain their end, which is fellowship with the Father, through the Son in the Spirit. Fellowship with God is thus the mystery of which the gospel is the open manifestation." See John Webster, "On Evangelical Ecclesiology," in *Confessing God: Essays in Christian Dogmatics II* (New York: T&T Clark, 2005), 153.

fullness of the mystery of God in redemption is disclosed among his people."[2]

The church arises only from the gospel. And a distorted church usually coincides with a distorted gospel. Whether it leads to such distortions or results from them, serious departures from the Bible's teaching about the church normally signify other, more central misunderstandings about the Christian faith.[3]

This is not to say that all differences in ecclesiology are tantamount to differences over the gospel itself. Honest Christians have long differed over a number of important issues in the church. But just because a matter is not essential for salvation does not mean that it's not important, or that it's not necessary for obedience. The color of church signs is not essential for Christian salvation, nor is believer's baptism. But everyone would agree that these two matters vary greatly in importance.

Perhaps the popular disinterest in ecclesiology results from the understanding that the church itself is not necessary for salvation. Cyprian of Carthage may well have said, "No one can have God for his father, who has not the church for his mother," but few would agree with this sentiment today.[4] The Church of Rome, in the Second Vatican Council, recognized that a normally competent adult is not required to self-consciously participate in the church for salvation.[5] And evangelical Protestants, who stress salvation by faith alone, seem to have even less use for the church, much less for studying the doctrine of the church.

It should not be this way. As John Stott said, "The church lies at the very center of the eternal purpose of God. It is not a divine afterthought. It is not an accident of history."[6] The church should be regarded as important

---

[2] James Montgomery Boice, *Foundations of the Christian Faith* (Downers Grove, IL: IVP; rev. ed., 1986), 565.
[3] See Jonathan Leeman, *The Church and the Surprising Offence of God's Love* (Wheaton, IL: Crossway), 17–19.
[4] Cyprian, *De Eccl. Cath. Unitate* (Oxford: Clarendon, 1971), chap. 6.
[5] *Lumem Gentium*, chap. 2, especially paragraph 16 (Austin Flannery, ed., *Vatican Council II* [Northport, NY: Costello Publishing Co., 1981], 367–68).
[6] John Stott, *The Living Church* (Downers Grove, IL: IVP, 2007), 19.

to Christians because of its importance to Christ. Christ founded the church (Matt 16:18), purchased it with his blood (Acts 20:28), and intimately identifies himself with it (Acts 9:4). The church is the body of Christ (1 Cor 12:12,27; Eph 1:22–23; 4:12; 5:20–30; Col 1:18,24; 3:15), the dwelling place of his Spirit (1 Cor 3:16–17; Eph 2:18,22; 4:4), and the chief instrument for glorifying God in the world (Ezek 36:22–38; Eph 3:10). Finally, the church is God's instrument for bringing both the gospel to the nations and a great host of redeemed humanity to himself (Luke 24:46–48; Rev 5:9).

More than once Jesus said that his people would demonstrate their love for him by obeying his commandments (John 14:15,23). And the obedience which interests him is not only individual but corporate. Together individuals in churches will go, disciple, baptize, teach to obey, love, remember, and commemorate his substitutionary death with the bread and the cup. Jan Hus, the fifteenth-century Bohemian reformer, put it this way: "Every earthly pilgrim ought faithfully . . . to love Jesus Christ, the Lord, the bridegroom of that church, and also the church herself, his bride."[7]

The enduring authority of Christ's commands should compel Christians to study the Bible's teaching on the church. Wrong ecclesial teaching and practices obscure the gospel while right ecclesial teaching and practices clarify it. To put it another way, Christian proclamation might make the gospel audible, but Christians living together in local congregations make the gospel visible (see John 13:34–35). The church is the gospel made visible.

Today many local churches are adrift in the shifting currents of pragmatism. They assume that the immediate response of non-Christians is the key indicator of success. At the same time, Christianity is being rapidly disowned in the culture at large. Evangelism is characterized as intolerant, and portions of biblical doctrine are classified as hate speech. In such antagonistic times the felt needs of non-Christians can hardly be considered reliable gauges, and conforming to the culture will mean a loss of the gospel itself. As long

[7] Jan Hus, *De Ecclesia: The Church*, trans. David Schley Schaff (New York: Charles Scribner's Sons, 1915), 1.

as quick numerical growth remains the primary indicator of church health, the truth will be compromised. Instead, churches must once again begin measuring success not in terms of numbers but in terms of fidelity to the Scriptures. William Carey served faithfully in India, and Adoniram Judson persevered in Burma not because they met immediate success or advertised themselves as "relevant."

This book is intended as a popular primer on the doctrine of the church, especially for Baptists but also, in so far as the arguments are convincing, for all of those who see Scripture alone to be the sufficient authority for the doctrine and life of the local church. The book grew out of a chapter I wrote almost a decade ago on the doctrine of the church.[8] The volume containing that chapter imposed a certain structure that is retained here. Part 1 considers the doctrine of the church biblically, part 2 historically, and part 3 systematically and practically. This structure does require some repetition with attendant advantages and disadvantages. For the less committed reader, the introduction is presented as an easier, more accessible summary of some of the arguments and conclusions of the book.

---

[8] Daniel Akin, ed., *A Theology for the Church* (Nashville: B&H, 2007); see chap. 13, "The Church," 766–856.

An Informal Introduction:
The Sufficiency of the Bible
for the Local Church

How is the gospel displayed in our lives as we live together with other Christians? What are we supposed to do? What are we supposed to believe? What are we supposed to do together in church? How are we supposed to make decisions? Lots of practical questions are faced by Christians when it comes to life in the local church, and Christians answer them differently—even if they preach the same gospel! How does that happen? What should we think about such differences?

Can you picture what I'm talking about? Suppose you are having a conversation with some Christian friends. And suppose that all of you agree about the gospel, the authority of Scripture, and numerous other theological particulars. But let's say also that they think there are some matters in the church's corporate life that God simply hasn't said anything about in his Word: On what day should we meet? What should we do when we meet? Should we all meet together, or can we have different services, maybe even different styles of services? Can we meet in different buildings, or in different parts of the city, or in different states, and still be one church? Is that OK? Does God care? Who should make decisions in the church? How are they to be made? Should we have members, or is that too exclusive? Most basic of all, how are we to make these decisions?

Over the centuries some Christians have answered such questions simply by reason and prudence. Others have let their experiences determine their answers, whether that's individual experience (an interior impression, a sense of God's leading) or corporate experience (church traditions). Still other churches answer the debatable questions by looking to what the people want, or to what the elders say, or to what the pastor says. For most churches the answers are found through some form of pragmatism—making the decision according to whatever works. The goal for many is to be sensitive to the particular culture that God has placed us in. The questions then become: How can we contextualize our message—to be Jews to the Jews and Gentiles to the Gentiles? Do we try to learn from the business world by adopting its best practices? Should the standards of creativity, innovation, productivity, and efficiency be our guides? What will help us reach the most people? What will best extend our influence?

A church's life, doctrine, worship, and even polity—all these are important issues. And they are so rarely addressed. In this book I hope to introduce the reader to what the Bible says about the nature and purpose of the church—what it is, what it is for, and what it does.

The Answer Is in the Bible

Everything we know about God and his will comes from God's own revelation. We only know the good news of Jesus Christ because God has revealed the truth about himself to us—and he has done that in his Word, the Bible. The truth of Christ is the means God's Spirit uses to reconcile us to himself. New life comes through the Word, just as Jesus prayed: "My prayer is not for them alone. I pray also for those who believe in me through their message" (John 17:20 NIV, used throughout this book). Notice that belief will come *through their message*.

And that is what happens in the remainder of the New Testament. For instance, Peter preached to Cornelius and his friends. Then, "While Peter was still speaking these words, the Holy Spirit came on all who heard the message" (Acts 10:44). Of course, God had told Cornelius to expect just this: Peter "will bring you a message through which you and all your household will be saved" (11:14).

Indeed, this is why Paul said that "faith comes from hearing the message" (Rom 10:17). Again, the preached Word creates life. Yet not only does the preached Word create the Christian life; it sustains and grows it. The Bible is our lifeline, our feast. Paul wrote toward the end of his life to Timothy:

> All Scripture is God-breathed and is useful for teaching, rebuking, correcting and training in righteousness, so that the man of God may be thoroughly equipped for every good work.
>
> In the presence of God and of Christ Jesus, who will judge the living and the dead, and in view of his appearing and his kingdom, I give you this charge: Preach the Word; be prepared in season and out of season; correct, rebuke and encourage—with great patience and careful instruction. (2 Tim 3:16–4:2)

This book attempts to provide such careful instruction so that we might understand and recover faithfulness to God's Word on something that is not essential for salvation but that is both important and necessary for obedience—what the local church is to be and to do. The Scriptures teaches us about all of life and doctrine, including how we should assemble for corporate worship and how we are to organize our corporate life together. The Bible certainly doesn't teach us everything. But neither does it teach us nothing. It should be our desire to search out everything that God has revealed about himself and then to joyfully accept it, adopt it, explore it, submit ourselves to it, and enjoy God's blessings in it.

As in every other topic, our regular practice as Christians should be to seek God's will in his Word, either by explicit command or by reasoning from principles in the Word. We want to see that the answer is in the Bible. Here are four introductory questions that will help us find God's will about the church.

What Should Churches Do?

The answer to this question is in the Bible. God made us. He knows what we were made for, and so we must look to his Word for discovering how we should live.

God has always been concerned with how the people called by his name would live. When God called Abram out of paganism (Gen 12:1–3), he called him *to believe* a promise, and that belief was to affect how Abram was *to live*. As Abraham's descendants multiplied in Egypt, God instructed his people, his assembly, on how to live. This is what the books of the Law—Exodus, Leviticus, Numbers, and Deuteronomy—are all about.

In the New Testament, Jesus promised his disciples that his authority would be with them till the end of the age (Matt 28:18–20). Was this promise and the accompanying instructions just for those initial apostles? Evidently not. They wouldn't be around till the end of the age. This promise and these instructions were also for those who would follow the apostles. They tell Christians and preachers and local churches how to live: we are to go, make disciples, baptize, and teach disciples to obey. God's Word has to do with life.

Paul also established churches and taught them—by his example and his letters—how to live (see Col 4:16). Churches should be marked out by the fruit of God's Spirit (Gal 5:22–23).

By direct command, example, implication, or principles, God's Word tells us everything we need to know about every aspect of following him in life—from dating to marriage, from working to grieving, from evangelizing to eating. What should churches do? The answer is in the Bible.

What Should Churches Believe?

The answer to this question is also in the Bible. God has revealed the truth about himself and about us. Therefore we are dependent on him for the good news and for everything else we need to know about God. In many ways a church is simply a group of people who are living lives of love (John 13:34–35) because they all agree on how they have been loved in Christ. Paul wrote:

> Now, brothers, I want to remind you of the gospel I preached to you, which you received and on which you have taken your stand. By this gospel you are saved, if you hold firmly to the word I preached to you. . . .
>
> For what I received I passed on to you as of first importance: that Christ died for our sins according to the Scriptures, that he was buried, that he was raised on the third day according to the Scriptures. (1 Cor 15:1–4)

Belief in this message is mandatory, both to be a Christian and to be a church. This is why Paul was so hard on the Galatians when they began to be tempted by other gospels (Gal 1:6–9).

What should we believe? Whether the matter is explicit (as with substitutionary atonement) or implicit (as with the Trinity or church membership), the answer is in the Bible.

How Should Churches Worship?

Having seen how this normally works in the Christian life, we can't be surprised that a third question finds the same answer. The answer to the third question is also in the Bible. In Scripture, God tells us how we should approach him in public worship. We read the Bible, sing the Bible, preach the Bible, pray the Bible, and see the Bible (in baptism and the Lord's Supper).

A church is not simply a group of people who believe the same gospel and live distinctly Spirit-led lives. We are also a group of people who come together regularly in order to worship God, in Jesus' words, "in spirit and in truth" (John 4:24). Jesus' words pertain to all of life, and that certainly includes those times when we assemble together. We are commanded in God's Word not to forsake these regular assemblies (Heb 10:25), so it is no surprise that God should instruct us in his Word what we are to do together.

Though creativity and innovation can play a secondary role, they should not be the principles which govern worship in the local church. Think about it: Christians are required to gather as churches. Therefore, when a church decides to implement a nonbiblical practice, it effectively requires Christians to approach God through that nonbiblical practice. The problem, of course, is that human beings have always proven to be unreliable guides for inventing ways to approach God. In the Bible human inventions were again and again counted as idolatrous. Consider the golden calf incident (Exodus 32). The Israelites sincerely desired to worship the God who had delivered them from Egypt, but then they went horribly wrong in their approach to God. Their disobedience, idolatry, and adultery showed itself in a grotesque distortion in their public worship. Throughout the Old Testament we find that how God's people approach God in worship is a matter of utmost seriousness—a matter about which God himself is not indifferent.[1] God has told us in his Word everything we need to know about what's necessary to approach him together.

One of the things that separated the false gods from the true God in the Old Testament is that the false gods were mute while the true God spoke. People can creatively devise how to approach a mute God, but they must listen to a speaking God. Jesus quoted Isaiah when he was correcting the distortions that the traditions of the Pharisees brought to the worship of God: "These people honor me with their lips, but their hearts are far from me. They worship me in vain; their teachings are but rules taught by men" (Mark 7:6–7; see Isa 29:13).

---

[1] Consider the examples of Cain (Gen 4:5), Nadab and Abihu (Lev 10:1; Num 3:4), and Uzzah (2 Sam 6:6–7). God condemned Israel's hypocritical worship (Amos 5:21–23) and the Corinthians' wrong celebrations (1 Cor 11:17).

Depravity makes us unreliable guides. We need God's self-revelation, or we are lost. Everything my own church does in our time together on Sunday morning we intend to do in obedience to God's Word.

- We begin with a scriptural call to worship so that we formally begin our time by hearing God address us in his Word.
- We may corporately recite various summary statements of what the Bible teaches, just as Rom 10:9 calls Christians to confess what they believe with their mouths.
- We sing hymns, psalms, and songs because we are commanded to (Rom 15:11; Eph 5:19; Col 3:16; Jas 5:13).
- We pray in praise (Heb 13:15); and we pray in intercession as instructed to (Jas 5:13–18; Eph 6:18).
- We read God's Word to one another (Rev 1:3; 1 Tim 4:13).
- We confess our sins (1 John 1:9), and then we remind ourselves from some passage of Scripture that God freely forgives our sin through Jesus Christ.
- We give financially as God instructed (Gal 6:6; 2 Tim 2:6) and as exampled in 1 Cor 16:2 (cf. the example of the Philippians in supporting Paul's ministry in Phil 4:15–16).
- We attend to preaching as God commanded (2 Tim 4:2) and as exampled throughout the book of Acts.
- We baptize as Jesus commanded (Matt 28:18–20), and we celebrate the Lord's Supper as he instructed (Luke 22:19).

How should we worship? The answer is in the Bible.

How Should Churches Live Together?

All this brings us to this final question, which gets at the matter of a church's polity or organization. Is there a diversity of church structures in the New Testament? Did the earliest churches start charismatic, as seemingly attested in

Acts and 1 and 2 Corinthians, but end up presbyterian, as some say is the case in 1 and 2 Timothy and Titus? Or does the New Testament bear witness to a consistent form of local church government?

God created the church, which means he has all authority in the church. He tells us what a church is and how it is to function. How should the church be organized? Again, the answer is in the Bible.

We need to know what a church is intended to be before we can evaluate what our churches are doing and what we should do going forward. Imagine trying to be a good husband or wife if you didn't know what marriage was. One kind of freedom comes with ignorance, and another (very different) kind comes with instruction. The freedom of ignorance is unconstrained but also unfruitful. Feel free to try to use that piano as a vacuum cleaner! The freedom that comes with instruction—using something in accordance with the purpose for which it was designed—is far more satisfying, like using a piano *to make music*.

The New Hampshire Confession of Faith defines a local church as follows:

> A visible church of Christ is a congregation of baptized believers, associated by covenant in the faith and fellowship of the Gospel; observing the ordinances of Christ; governed by His laws; and exercising the gifts, rights, and privileges invested in them by His word; that its only scriptural officers are Bishops or Pastors, and Deacons, whose qualifications, claims, and duties are defined in the Epistles to Timothy and Titus.

A church is governed by Christ's laws and lives in obedience to his teachings. In other words the Bible tells churches how to function. This is what the Westminster Confession said as well:

> The whole counsel of God, concerning all things necessary for His own glory, man's salvation, faith and life, is either expressly set down in Scripture, or by

good and necessary consequence may be deduced
from Scripture: unto which nothing at any time is to
be added, whether by new revelations of the Spirit, or
traditions of men. (WCF 1.6; cf. 2 Tim 3:15–17; Gal
1:8–9; 2 Thess 2:2)

Objections

I realize that many evangelicals today may not accept
the idea that the Bible tells us how we are to organize our
churches. There are a few reasons for this. Many question
whether the Bible teaches on this at all, either explicitly or
implicitly. In most evangelical and even Baptist seminaries
today, it is suggested that there is no consistent pattern of
polity in the New Testament.[2] (If that has been your assumption, ask yourself what you would do if there *were* teachings
on this in the Bible.) Others point out that Scripture can
be deemed "sufficient" without specifically addressing every
question that might pop into our minds. Or they say that
people imagine things and read them into the Bible.

Of course, these last two points are certainly true. But
to observe that Scripture is "sufficient" is to observe that it's
sufficient for helping us do whatever God would have us do.
And in the Bible God demonstrates that he does care about
the organization and structure of the local church. He has
established different kinds of people in the church, including
teachers and administrators (1 Cor 12:28). He seems to be
interested in "how orderly" a church is (Col 2:5). And God
calls churches to consider carefully their members' lives and
professions of faith (Matt 18:15–17; 1 Cor 5; cf. 1 John 4:1–3).

Others may reject the whole conversation, saying that
it is not important. There is almost an impatience with
anything that is nonessential. Too often Christians today
have only two gears on their theological bike: essential and

---

[2] One example of this from an earlier generation would be this typical statement
"As to 'polity,' New Testament roots for Episcopal, presbyterian, and congregational models are traceable; but there is no clear-cut case for the dominance of
any," Frank Stagg, "The New Testament Doctrine of the Church," *The Theological
Educator* 12, no. 1 (Fall 1981): 48.

unimportant. If something is not essential for salvation, it is treated as unimportant and therefore dismissable. But the Bible presents us with a number of matters that are not essential for salvation but which nonetheless are important, even necessary, for obedience to God's Word. And these commands are not arbitrary. Obeying them bears good fruit. Questions of polity and organization fall into this category. In the life of a local church, they can sometimes become crucially important for the church's health and even survival.

One last objection to consider may be simply, "Nobody thinks this!" But this last object is historically unfounded. Christians have long thought about such matters, which is why whole denominations are called Presbyterian or Congregational or Methodist or Episcopalian, designations that refer to how these churches do things. John Bunyan and Jonathan Edwards, John Wesley and C. H. Spurgeon—all of them believed that the Bible taught us how we should organize our churches. One could even say that New England was founded over such matters. So were Baptist churches. Many Christians before us have thought these matters were important because they saw them in the Bible.

Speaking for the congregation I serve, our church agrees with the Christians before us, including the ones who founded our local congregation in the 1870s, that the Bible does teach about these matters. We believe these matters are important enough to consider carefully and to study Scripture carefully, expecting to find some answers on how we are to structure our lives together in the local church. We aim to fashion our church structure and practices on the explicit and implicit teaching of the Bible found in commands and examples.[3]

Example 1: Who Is the Church?

Having established the basic principle of being directed by Scripture, and having considered some popular objections

---

[3] The question of which examples are to be followed is both important and sometimes unclear. There is a small, middle category of examples (and even some commands) that were temporary and situational (like greeting one another with a holy kiss), and yet even they embodied larger, abiding principles. Unending discussion can occur on these kinds of examples.

to it, let's turn now to three examples of how the Bible's teaching on polity matters, even if many Christians today rarely seem to understand or appreciate what the Bible says here.

The first and most basic matter of church polity is, "Who is the church?" And the answer is fairly simple: the members comprise the local church. And just as the Bible determines what a congregation believes, so it also determines who has the final say on who its own members are.

- In Matt 18:15–20, Jesus taught that if people do not repent of their sins they must be excluded from the local church. And he called the church to do this.
- In 1 Corinthians 5, Paul followed Jesus' teaching. He told the whole local church—not just the elders—to expel an unrepentant sinner from their number.
- In 2 Cor 2:6, Paul referred to a punishment inflicted on a straying member by "the majority." Again, he is not writing to the elders but to the congregation as a whole.

In these passages on discipline, the meaning of membership is seen. Discipline draws a circle around the membership of the church. Careful practices of membership and discipline are meant to mark off the church from the world and thereby define and display the gospel.

Churches which practice no formal membership and discipline at least make it more difficult for the believers who are part of it to follow Christ and more difficult for those elders to know for whom they are to give an account (Heb 13:17). In fact, I would go a step further and say that churches which practice no self-conscious membership are in sin since Christians cannot follow basic biblical commands without it. According to the New Testament, church leaders need to know who is and who is not a member of the congregation. And perhaps even more important, Christians need to know this—for their own souls' sake!

Example 2: Who Is Finally Responsible?

A second topic of polity which the Bible addresses is, "Who is finally responsible for what happens in a church?" The last example touched on this, but I want to make it explicit: the New Testament gives ultimate responsibility to the congregation.

It appears to give final responsibility to the congregation in matters of discipline and, by implication, membership. Consider again the three passages listed above, such as 2 Cor 2:6, where a majority made the decision to excommunicate the sinning member. The church made the decision.

The Bible also seems to give ultimate authority to the congregation in matters of doctrine and, by implication, the selection of leaders. This is evidenced, for instance, by Paul's appeal to the Galatian congregations to trust their own judgment over that of an apostle or even an angel, should an apostle or angel ever attempt to alter the content of the good news (Gal 1:6–9). Again, it is not the elders Paul called to act. In another letter he blamed churches for gathering around them a great number of teachers to say what their itching ears wanted to hear (2 Tim 4:3). Surely this is an example of congregational authority poorly used. The apostle John called on another church to do just the opposite—exercise its responsibility carefully by taking heed to the teaching it received (2 John 10–11).

In these examples the New Testament shows clearly that it was not something external to the local church, like an association of churches or a general assembly or a bishop, that had final responsibility for what happened in a local church. It was the congregation itself. Nor was final responsibility held by some subset of the membership, like a council or the elders or a pastor. Though elders do have increased accountability due to their public teaching of the Word (Jas 3:1), such decisions are finally matters of the congregation's responsibility.

This final responsibility of the congregation need not undermine pastoral leadership. Rather, it can both reinforce it and guard against abuses of it. In a healthy church the congregation will always (or almost always) support the elders. They will have the same understanding of Scripture and will generally take the same view of practical matters. The New Testament's congregational responsibility is not like a New England town meeting, with no elders to lead them. Normally congregations should joyfully submit to the church's pastors and elders. However, they should also maintain the ability to reject what the elders might bring to the members. This is an important, biblical, and sometimes even gospel-saving emergency break, which has been revealed by God in his Word.

Example 3: Should Churches Have Multiple Leaders?

This question raises one more example of what the Bible teaches on church polity. If talk about what the Bible teaches on church structure is met with skepticism by many evangelicals today, surely claims about the nature and number of officers in a church follow suit.

With all due respect to those who would disagree, I think the Bible clearly teaches that local congregations should be led by a plurality of elders. This is the consistent pattern of churches in the New Testament. For instance, Paul told Timothy to appoint them at the churches in every town (in Titus 1:5; cf. Acts 14:23). He addressed the elders (or "overseers") as a group at the church in Philippi (Phil 1:1). And he did the same with the elders of the church in Ephesus (Acts 20:17). James also referred to "the elders of the church" (Jas 5:14). In short, nowhere does the New Testament say something like, "Submit to *the elder* in your church." Instead, the word always occurs in the plural. The example is uniform (cf. the references to the elders in the church in Jerusalem in Acts 11:30; 15:2; 21:18). If Paul and the apostles encouraged and instructed the earliest churches to follow this pattern, it would seem we should follow this pattern as well.[4]

---

[4] As William Williams, founding professor of church history at the Southern Baptist Theological Seminary, put it, "Are we under obligation to adopt that polity which divine wisdom has pointed out to be the best adapted to promote the ends of church organization, or may we feel at liberty to change it or to substitute some other, according to our views of fitness and expediency?" ("Apostolical Church

Such conclusions are important because God has revealed his will for us on these matters. The Christian response should be to hear and heed his Word. William Ames, author of the theology text used for decades at Harvard College, *Marrow of Divinity*, asserted just this very thing:

> Man . . . does not have power either to take away any of those things which Christ has given his church or to add things of like kind. Yet in every way he can and ought to make certain that the things which Christ has ordained are furthered and strengthened. . . . [Because Christ alone is the head of the church] the church may not properly make new laws for itself for instituting new things. It ought to take care only to find out the will of Christ clearly and observe his ordinances decently and with order, with greatest edification resulting.[5]

A Few More Questions

Insisting that Scripture governs what a local church is and does might raise a few more questions for readers, such as the following.

Do We Have to Be Inflexible on Everything?

No. Many other issues of polity and organization allow for flexibility and for consideration to be given to the particulars of time, place, and even culture. Examples include whether a church has a Sunday evening gathering, committees, Sunday school, or task-specific deacons. Scripture speaks to none of these directly, and the local congregation has the liberty to address such questions for its own edification.

Polity," in *Polity: Biblical Arguments on How to Conduct Church Life*, ed. Mark Dever [Washington, DC: Center for Church Reform, 2001], 546).
[5] William Ames, *Marrow of Divinity* (1634; repr., Boston: United Church Press, 1968), 181.

Does Lacking Any of These Things Mean That a Church Is Not Really a Church?

Here's a simple way Christians in the past have thought about this question: Churches which preach the gospel are true churches; churches which do not are not. Churches that preach the gospel but possess a biblically deficient form of polity can be considered "true" but "irregular" churches. They are "irregular" since they are not organized according to the rule—God's rule, the rule of his Word. The role of good pastors is then to move their congregations—as they should their own lives—toward increasing conformity to God's Word, even if such work is slow.

Can Christians Share Fellowship Even When They Disagree on These Kinds of Polity Matters?

Assuming that Christians share the gospel, they should be able to enjoy some form of fellowship, even if their polity differences mean they will belong to different churches. We may be convinced that a brother or a sister is in error, but we should show the same kindness to them that we hope they will show to us in our mistakes. This is precisely how Paul instructed the Roman Christians to deal with one another when disagreeing over secondary issues (Romans 14).

Why Do Some Christians See More About Polity in Scripture Than Others Do?

This is puzzling, but polity certainly wouldn't be the only area in which Christians maintain diverse interpretations. Perhaps some churches have been shown it by those who have gone before; they have read older writers. The important thing is that we should not approach such matters by arguing but by pointing to the Bible and then letting the Bible do its work. By this token the goal of this book is not so much to encourage Christians to draw lines between themselves and other Christians but to draw out clearly the path upon which we will walk.

So God created the church, and God the author has authority. In his Word he tells us what a church is and some important things about how a church is to function.

Conclusion

For some this introduction has already gone too deep. For others the importance of this topic will draw them into the pages that follow and through them, it is hoped, to the Scriptures and to the reflections of many others who have gone before. Suffice it to say that this topic is worth the study. Indeed, it is far more important than many realize.

My hope is that the reader sees how Scripture's beautiful sufficiency frees us from the tyranny of mere human opinion. God has revealed himself by his Word. He is speaking to us, preparing us to represent him today and to see him tomorrow! A congregation of regenerate members—fulfilling the responsibilities given to us by Christ himself in his Word, regularly meeting together, led by a body of godly elders—is the picture that God has given us in his Word of his church—what he calls his "household," a household bought with his own blood (1 Tim 3:15; Acts 20:28; cf. Mark 3:31–35).

Finally, consider what God is doing through the church. Paul said, "His intent was that now, through the church, the manifold wisdom of God should be made known to the rulers and authorities in the heavenly realms, according to his eternal purpose which he accomplished in Christ Jesus our Lord" (Eph 3:10–11). This is what God is doing! As such, our concern should be like Paul's—"that the church manifest and display the glory of God, thus vindicating God's character against all the slander of demonic realms, the slander that God is not worth living for. God has entrusted to his church the glory of his own name."[6]

For the sake of his name, then, God marshals us as his mighty army. Here's how one pastor put it in 1589:

> This holy army of saints, is marshaled here in earth by these officers, under the conduct of their glorious emperor Christ, that victorious Michael. Thus it marcheth in this most heavenly order, and gracious array, against all enemies both bodily and ghostly.

---

[6] Mark Ross, "An Address at the PCA Convocation on Revival."

Peaceable in itself as Jerusalem, terrible unto them as an army with banners, triumphing over their tyranny with patience, their cruelty with meekness, and over death itself with dying. Thus through the blood of that spotless lamb, and that word of their testimony, they are more than conquerors, bruising the head of the serpent; yea, through the power of the Word, they have power to cast down Satan like lightning: to tread upon serpents and scorpions: to cast down strongholds, and every thing that exalteth itself against God. The gates of hell and all the principalities and powers of the world, shall not prevail against it.[7]

This is the glorious subject of this book.

---

[7] Henry Barrow, "A True Description of the Visible Church" reprinted in Iain Murray, ed., *The Reformation of the Church: A Collection of Reformed and Puritan Documents on Church Issues* (Carlisle, PA: Banner of Truth Trust, 1965), 200–201.

Part 1

What Does the Bible Say?

1

The Nature of the Church

The church is the body of people called by God's grace through faith in Christ to glorify him together by serving him in his world.[1]

The People of God in the Old Testament: Israel

In order to understand the church in the full richness of God's revealed truth, we must examine both the Old and New Testaments. Christians may sometimes use the phrase "a New Testament church," but the shape of the visible church

---

[1] A great definition of the church was given by Henry Barrow in 1589: "This church as it is universally understood, containeth in it all the elect of God that have been, are, or shall be. But being considered more particularly, as it is seen in this present world, it consisteth of a company and fellowship of faithful and holy people gathered together in the name of Christ Jesus, their only king, priest, and prophet, worshipping him aright, being peacably and quietely governed by his officers and laws, keeping the unity of faith in the bond of peace and love unfeigned" (Henry Barrow, "A True Description of the Visible Church," reprinted in Iain Murray, ed., *The Reformation of the Church: A Collection of Reformed and Puritan Documents on Church Issues* [Carlisle, PA: Banner of Truth Trust, 1965], 196). For a typical Baptist definition of the church, see the definition given by the Charleston Association: "A particular gospel church consists of a company of saints incorporated by a special covenant into one distinct body, and meeting together in one place, for the enjoyment of fellowship with each other and with Christ their head, in all his institutions, to their mutual edification and the glory of God through the Spirit," quoted in Mark Dever, "A Summary of Church Discipline," *Polity: Biblical Arguments in How to Conduct Church Life* (Washington, DC: Center for Church Reform [9Marks Ministries], 2001), 118.

today bears a clear continuity—though not identity—with the visible people of God in the Old Testament.

God's eternal plan has always been to display his glory not just through individuals but through a corporate body. In creation God created not one person but two, and two who have the ability to reproduce more. In the flood God saved not one person but several families. In Genesis 12 God called Abram and promised that Abram's descendents would be as numerous as the stars in the sky or the sand on the seashore. In Exodus God dealt not only with Moses but with the nation of Israel—12 tribes comprised of hundreds of thousands of people yet bearing one corporate identity (see Exod 15:13–16). He gave laws and ceremonies that should be worked out not only in the lives of individuals but also in the life of the whole people.

In the Old Testament, Israel is called God's son (Exod 4:22), his spouse (Ezek 16:6–14), the apple of his eye (Deut 32:10), his vine (Isa 5:1–7; Nah 2:2), and his flock (Ezek 34:4). Through these names God foreshadowed the work he would eventually do through Christ and his church.

Etymologically, a connection exists between the Old Testament word for "assembly," qahal (קָהָל) and the New Testament word translated "church," ekklesia (ἐκκλησία). The Greek version of the Old Testament, the Septuagint, translates qahal in Deut 4:10 and elsewhere with ekklesia.[2] And this word for assembly, qahal, is closely bound up in the Old Testament with the Lord's distinct people Israel. The rich association between the assembly of God and the distinct people of God in the Old Testament qahal then carries over to the New Testament ekklesia, the church. The church is literally an assembly (see Heb 10:25). It is God's assembly because God dwells with the church. And the church is comprised of people who are beginning to know the reversal of the effects of the fall. So members of both Israel and the church receive a glimpse of the glory which awaits God's people.

Isaiah saw and heard seraphim calling to one another, "Holy, holy, holy is the LORD Almighty; the whole earth is

---

[2] Cf. Deut 4:10; Acts 7:38.

full of his glory" (Isa 6:3). John then encountered what appears to be the same heavenly assembly when he heard the angels, living creatures, and elders singing, "Worthy is the Lamb, who was slain, to receive power and wealth and wisdom and strength and honor and glory and praise!" (Rev 5:12). Though Isaiah and John's visions are unique, Paul told the Corinthians that unbelievers would perceive this same God at work among them: "God is really among you" (1 Cor 14:25). Heaven appears on earth in God's assembly, the church.

Christians divide over how closely Israel should be identified with the church.[3] The New Testament identities Israel and the church with each other in one place only, where Paul refers to "all who follow this rule" in the Galatian church with the title "the Israel of God" (Gal 6:16). While some suggest that "Israel of God" refers specifically to the Jews who belong to the predominantly Gentile churches in Galatia, others are convinced that in the same letter Paul refers to all Christians, Jew and Gentile, as "Abraham's seed" (Gal 3:29), indicating the link between Israel and church is deliberate.

Distinctions between the Old and New Testament people of God are obvious. God's people in the Old Testament are ethnically distinct; in the New Testament they are ethnically mixed. In the Old they live under their own government with God-given laws; in the New they live among the rulers of the nations. In the Old they are required to circumcise their male offspring; in the New they are required to baptize all believers. What accounts for the change in the move from the Old Testament to the New? Jesus fulfilled the explicit promises of God in the Old Testament and even of patterns found there. He is the fulfillment of the temple and its priesthood, of the land and its rulers, even of the nation of Israel as a son of God.

Continuities between Israel and the church are more debated. Acts 15 is a particularly significant passage on this question. At the Jerusalem Council, James quoted a prophesy from Amos 9:11–12 which promises that David's fallen

---

[3] This distinction is fundamental to dispensationalism.

tent would be restored and that Israel would come to possess the nations that bear the Lord's name. James affirmed that this prophecy points toward the church's present circumstances and the recent influx of Gentile believers. The "apostles and elders" (Acts 15:6), meeting to consider precisely the question of the Gentile believers, seem to accept the recent influx of Gentile believers into the church as a fulfillment of the prophecy about Gentiles coming to Israel.[4]

Though Israel and the church are not identical, they are closely related, and they are related through Jesus Christ (see Eph 2:12–13). Israel was called to be the Lord's servant but was unfaithful to him. Jesus, on the other hand, is a faithful servant (see Matt 4:1–11). The temples of Solomon and Ezra, as well as in Ezekiel's vision, all point toward Jesus Christ, whose body constitutes the supreme earthly tabernacle for God's Spirit. The land of Israel, especially the city of Jerusalem, points toward the redemption of the whole earth. Heaven itself is referred to as the new Jerusalem. The multinational church fulfills the promises given to the 12 tribes (see Revelation 7). And the law of the Old Testament finds its fulfillment in Christ (see Matt 5:17). Christ is the fulfillment of all that Israel points toward (see 2 Cor 1:20), and the church is Christ's body.

At the very least, it must be said that God has consistently had a plan to glorify his name through groups of people he chose and took as his own.[5] Hence, one writer observed, "The story of the church begins with Israel, the Old Testament people of God."[6]

---

[4] This would also be similar to the way the writer to the Hebrews in Hebrews 8 appears to regard the prophesy in Jeremiah 31 concerning the houses of Judah and Israel as fulfilled in the church.
[5] See George Eldon Ladd, *The Gospel of the Kingdom* (Grand Rapids: Eerdmans, 1959), 120. For contrasting views see the traditional dispensationalist position represented by John F. Walvoord, *The Millennial Kingdom* (Grand Rapids: Zondervan, 1959). For the progressive dispensational position, see Craig Blaising and Darrell Bock, eds. *Dispensationalism, Israel and the Church* (Grand Rapids: Zondervan, 1992); and Robert Saucy, *The Case for Progressive Dispensationalism* (Grand Rapids: Zondervan, 1993). For the reformed position, see O. Palmer Robertson, *The Israel of God* (Phillipsburg: P&R, 2000); and Robert Reymond, *A New Systematic Theology of the Christian Faith* (Nashville: Thomas Nelson, 1998), 503–44.
[6] Edmund Clowney, *The Church* (Downers Grove, IL: IVP, 1995), 28. Clowney's book is one of the best introductions in print to the doctrine of the church.

The People of God in the New Testament: The Church

Explicit Teaching

At one particularly low point in the moral degeneration of Israel, the writer of Judges described the nation as "the people of God" (עַם הָאֱלֹהִים Judg 20:2; see 2 Sam 14:13). The Greek equivalent of this phrase (τῷ λαῷ τοῦ θεοῦ) is used by the writer of Hebrews to describe the people of Israel with whom Moses identified himself instead of identifying himself with Pharaoh's household (Heb 11:25), and he had used this same phrase earlier to refer to Christians (4:9). Peter also employed this phrase, telling his readers, "Once you were not a people, but now you are the people of God [λαὸς θεοῦ]" (1 Pet 2:10). And John the Baptist came "to make ready a people prepared for the Lord" (Luke 1:17).

Meanings of *Ekklesia*

In the New Testament, the English word *church* can be used to describe both a local congregation or all Christians everywhere. In contemporary use the word is also used to describe buildings and denominations. In these latter ways the English word *church* does not exactly parallel the Greek word in the New Testament.[7]

The word translated "church" is *ekklesia,* which occurs 114 times in the New Testament.[8] No other Greek word is translated "church" in English versions. But *ekklesia* was used in the New Testament period to describe more than the gatherings of Christians. The word was often used in Greek cities to refer to assemblies called to perform specific tasks. In Acts 7:38 and Heb 2:12, *ekklesia* is used to describe Old Testament assemblies. Luke uses *ekklesia* three times to describe the riot that gathers in an amphitheater in Ephesus to deal with Paul (Acts 19:32,39,41). The remaining 109

---

[7] William Tyndale regularly translated *ekklesia* as "congregation."
[8] Three times in Matthew, 20 in Acts, 66 in Paul's writings, once in Hebrews, once in James, three in 3 John, and 20 in Revelation.

uses of the word in the New Testament refer to a Christian assembly.

Uses of Ekklesia

Jesus Christ founded his own assembly, his own church.[9] According to Matthew's Gospel, Jesus first names his New Testament people as "my church" (16:18). As Adam named his bride, so Christ names the church. Yet Jesus only refers to the church twice in his recorded teaching (Matt 16:18; 18:17). Since Jesus understood that he was the Messiah, his references to his church almost certainly contain the Hebrew idea of *qahal* or "assembly."[10] The Messiah was expected to establish his Messianic assembly, and so throughout the Gospels Christ marks out those who are faithful to recognize and follow him.

The book of Acts usually refers to specific local gatherings with the word *ekklesia*,[11] such as the assemblies in Jerusalem, Antioch, Derbe, Lystra, and Ephesus. These churches met and sent missionaries (see 15:3). Luke also quoted Paul as saying that the church was bought with God's "own blood" (Acts 20:28).

Paul often referred to the church (or churches) of God[12] or the church (or churches) of Christ.[13] He identified himself as being a former persecutor of the church (Phil 3:6; see 1 Cor 15:9). And his apostolic ministry centered on planting churches and building up churches. Paul's letters (particularly to the Corinthians) are filled with instructions to the early Christians about their behavior in their assemblies. One scholar therefore observed, "When he speaks of ἐκκλησία, [Paul] normally thinks first of the concrete

---

[9] This is contra the influential position expressed by Alfred Loisy in the early twentieth century that "Jesus foretold the kingdom, and it was the church that came" (Loisy, *The Gospel and the Church* [repr.; Philadelphia, Fortress Press 1976], 166).
[10] The Septuagint translates the Hebrew word *qahal* (קָהָל) with the Greek word *ekklesia* (ἐκκλησία) 77 times.
[11] The one exception to this may be in Acts 9:31. But because this usage is unique, perhaps this is the result of the one church of Jerusalem, which had been scattered, still being referred to as a unit.
[12] E.g., 1 Cor 1:2; 10:32; 11:16,22; 15:9; 2 Cor 1:1; Gal 1:13; 1 Thess 2:14; 2 Thess 1:4.
[13] E.g., Rom 16:16; Gal 1:22.

assembly of those who have been baptized at a specific place. . . . Ecclesiological statements that lead beyond the level of the local assembly are rare in Paul's letters."[14] In Ephesians and Colossians, Paul intimately related and identified Christ with the churches (e.g., Eph 2:20; 3:10–12; 4:15; Col 1:17–18,24; 2:10), particularly by using the language of husband/wife and head/body to describe Christ's relationship to the church (Col 3:18–19; Eph 5:22–33).

General Epistles

The book of Hebrews mentions the church once (12:23), referring to an earthly assembly with a heavenly destiny.[15] James 5:14 refers to a local church and its elders. Both 2 John and 3 John picture a particular congregation and its struggles with false teachers and leaders. Outside of Paul and Acts, the book of Revelation has more occurrences of *ekklesia* than any other book in the New Testament. Except for 22:16, these all occur in the first three chapters. The word is used 14 times in these opening chapters in a formula format to either begin or conclude a separate letter to each of the seven churches.[16] And then Jesus stated that he has sent his angel "to give you this testimony for the churches." So the message of this book from chapters 4 through 22 is meant for the local churches.

Images and Names of the Church

Much of the New Testament's teaching about the nature of the church itself can be derived from the images used for the church. Paul Minear in his classic work *Images of the Church in the New Testament* points to 96 images for the church in the New Testament.[17] While the number 96 may not be precisely correct, said Roman Catholic theologian Avery Dulles in his more recent work *Models of the Church,* he agreed that the New Testament authors use a

---

[14] J. Roloff, "ἐκκλησία," in *Exegetical Dictionary of the New Testament,* vol. 1, eds. Horst Balz and Gerhard Schneider (Grand Rapids: Eerdmans, 1990), 412–13.
[15] Heb 2:12 as a reference to an Old Testament assembly was mentioned earlier.
[16] See Rev 2:1,7,8,11,12,17,18,29; 3:1,6,7,13,14,22.
[17] Paul S. Minear, *Images of the Church in the New Testament* (Philadelphia: Westminster, 1960).

large number of images.[18] God has inspired multiple images, each of which offers a different perspective, and none of which should so dominate our conception of the church that the depth and texture of understanding is lost. Though all are inspired, they are not interchangeable, nor are they all as comprehensive in their presentation of the nature and purpose of the church.[19] The great images are familiar: the church as the people of God, the new creation, the fellowship or communion in faith, and of course, the body of Christ.

The richness of descriptions of the church teaches us that no single image can comprehend all aspects of the church. The church is the herald of the gospel (as in Acts). The church is the obedient servant (drawing from Isaiah). The church is the bride of Christ (as in Revelation 19 and 21). The church is a building (1 Pet 2:5; Eph 2:21), and the church is a temple (1 Cor 3:16; 2 Cor 6:16; Eph 2:19–22; 1 Pet 2:4–8). The church is the community of people who live in the last days inaugurated by Christ's earthly ministry and the coming of the Spirit. Many other minor images of the church could be listed, such as "the salt of the earth" (Matt 5:13) or "a letter from Christ" (2 Cor 3:3). The church is the family of believers (Gal 6:10; cf. Mark 3:31–35) and "the family of God" (1 Pet 4:17). But particular consideration should be given to four major image clusters mentioned above.[20]

First, the church is the people of God. This image has already been considered in the discussion of Old Testament background. It is also present in the New Testament. Peter used the title to encourage the readers of his first epistle (1 Pet 2:9–10; see Rom 9:25–26; Hos 1:9–10; 2:23). These

---

[18] Avery Dulles, *Models of the Church*, 2nd ed. (New York: Image, 1987).

[19] The present book refers to the comprehensive ends and goals of God for the church by the word "purpose" and the specific subset of that which relates to the church being sent out into the world by the word "mission." For more on this helpful distinction, see Kevin DeYoung and Greg Gilbert, *What Is the Mission of the Church?* (Wheaton, IL: Crossway, 2011), esp. 17–20.

[20] Another common way to categorize the various New Testament images of the church has been to use the trinitarian structure of the people of God, the body of Christ, and the dwelling of the Spirit. So Hans Kung, *The Church*, trans. Ray and Rosaleen Ockenden (Tunbridge Wells, England: Search Press, 1968), 107–260; Dale Moody, *The Word of Truth* (Grand Rapids: Eerdmans, 1981), 440–48; Clowney, *The Church*, 27–70; Millard Erickson, *Christian Theology*, 2nd ed. (Grand Rapids: Baker, 1998), 1044–51.

young Christians were struggling with the at-times painful distinction being made between their identity in Christ and others around them. Peter's language of a temple, constituted by the living stones of Christian lives with Christ himself as cornerstone (1 Pet 2:4–6), reminded these discouraged Christians that they are the people of God, the product of God's gracious work of transforming them into an integrated reality—a single people. The people of God are based on him and his act, deriving their identity from him uniquely. Many connections made with the Old Testament—the seed of Abraham (Gal 3:29), the holy nation (1 Pet 2:9), Israel (Romans 9–11)—confirm the status of the church as the people of God.

Second, the church is the new creation. Many evangelical Christians think of the new creation in connection with the explicit language of Paul in 2 Cor 5:17: "If anyone is in Christ, he is a new creation; the old has gone, the new has come!" They immediately associate this with the conversion of an individual believer. But the new creation image is corporate as well as individual. In the New Testament, Christ's resurrection is the firstfruits from among the dead (see 1 Cor 15:20–23). And in his resurrection, the great final resurrection has begun. In these references all the kingdom of God images become relevant. God is granting a new beginning, a new creation through Christ, in which the people of God increasingly conform to the kingdom or rule of God.

A third major image cluster used for the church is centered around the idea of fellowship. The salutations in Paul's letters present the Christians whom he was addressing as sharing particular points of distinctiveness from the world around them. So in 1 Cor 1:2, Paul wrote, "To the church of God in Corinth, to those sanctified in Christ Jesus and called to be holy, together with all those everywhere who call on the name of our Lord Jesus Christ—their Lord and ours." The Corinthian Christians, like Christians everywhere, share the status of being set apart for God's special purposes. Likewise, Christians everywhere are called together to holiness. Jesus prayed for his followers to know such a fellowship (see John 17), and such a fellowship we find throughout

Acts and the letters. Much of the material in the letters represents the working out of this common life, as the authors encouraged believers to interact in a way that both brings glory to God and reflects their shared status as Christ's followers, Christ's disciples, and Christ's friends (Luke 12:4; John 15:15).

Ultimately, fellowship among Christians in the church is based on the Christian's covenantal union with Christ. According to the New Testament, therefore, Christians live with Christ, suffer with Christ, are crucified with Christ, die with Christ, will be raised with Christ, and are glorified with Christ. Christ's life, sufferings, death, resurrection, and glory become theirs through their membership in his new covenant.

The final, and perhaps best known, image used to characterize the church is the body of Christ. Paul stated, "Because there is one loaf, we, who are many, are one body, for we all partake of the one loaf" (1 Cor 10:17). He used the image at great length in 1 Corinthians 12 to describe the diversity of gifts within the one body of the church. In Eph 3:6, Paul argued that Jewish and Gentile believers belong to the same body. Did Paul invent this image? No, it was given to him at his conversion, when the risen Christ asked him, "Saul, Saul, why do you persecute me?" (Acts 9:4).

The Church and the Kingdom of God

One other image in the New Testament worth considering briefly is the kingdom of God, a metaphor which refers to God's rule or reign. Jesus Christ taught his followers to pray "Our Father in heaven, hallowed be your name, your kingdom come" (Matt 6:9–10). The question which naturally arises in our context is whether or not the kingdom is identical with the church. Is it one more image like the others? Though Roman Catholic theology tends to identify church and kingdom, Scripture makes a distinction between the reign of God (present and coming) and the church. The church in fact comprises the people of the kingdom, as George Eldon Ladd explained:

> The Kingdom is not identified with its subjects. They are the people of God's rule who enter it, live under it, and are governed by it. The church is the community of the Kingdom but never the Kingdom itself. Jesus' disciples belong to the Kingdom as the Kingdom belongs to them; but they are not the Kingdom. The Kingdom is the rule of God; the church is a society of man.[21]

This kingdom is not a matter of geography or national politics; it is rather a matter of recognizing God's authority and living under it. One cannot speak biblically of the kingdom apart from the king.[22] In the book of Acts, the apostles do not preach the church, they preach the kingdom—God's reign.[23]

Thus, the church is the *koinonia* or "fellowship" of people who have accepted and entered into the reign of God. This reign is not entered into by nations, or even families, but by individuals (see Mark 3:31–35; cf. Matt 10:37). In Jesus' parable of the tenants (Matt 21:33–40), the kingdom of God is taken from the Jews and given to a people "who will produce its fruit" (v. 43; see Acts 28:26–28; 1 Thess 2:16). The relationship between the kingdom and the church can therefore be defined: *the kingdom of God creates the church*. True Christians "constitute a Kingdom in their relation to God in Christ as their Ruler, and a Church in their separateness from the world in devotion to God, and in their organic union with one another."[24]

Matthew 16:19 is a particularly important text for understanding the relation between the kingdom and the church. Jesus promised to give "the keys of the kingdom of heaven." Whatever he precisely means by promising the keys of the kingdom, the power of the kingdom is certainly being entrusted to the church. "The kingdom is God's deed. It has

---

[21] George Eldon Ladd, *A Theology of the New Testament*, rev. ed. (Grand Rapids: Eerdmans, 1993), 111. Cf. Roman Catholic theologian Hans Kung's criticism of his church's teaching on this point in his book *The Church*, 92–93.

[22] For a good summary of this, see Kevin DeYoung and Greg Gilbert, *What Is the Mission of the Church?* (Wheaton, IL: Crossway, 2011), 115–39.

[23] E.g., Philip's preaching in Acts 8:12 and Paul's in Acts 19:8 or 28:23.

[24] Louis Berkhof, *Systematic Theology* (Grand Rapids: Eerdmans, 1938), 569.

come into the world in Christ; it works in the world through the church. When the church has proclaimed the gospel of the kingdom in all the world as witness to all nations, Christ will return (Matt 24:14) and bring the kingdom in glory."[25]

---

[25] George Eldon Ladd, "Kingdom of God," in *Evangelical Dictionary of Theology*, 2nd ed., ed. Walter Elwell (Grand Rapids: Baker, 2001), 611; cf. Berkhof, 568–70. For more on the keys, see Jonathan Leeman, *The Church and the Surprising Offense of God's Love* (Wheaton, IL: Crossway, 2010), esp. 182–95.

2

The Attributes of the Church:
One, Holy, Universal, Apostolic

T he church reflects the character of God. The Niceno-Constantinopolitan Creed, fashioned by the Council of Constantinople in AD 381, affirms that Christians believe in "one, holy, universal and apostolic church." These four adjectives (*notae ecclesiae*) have been used historically to summarize biblical teaching on the church.[1] The church is one, holy, universal, and apostolic as a reflection of God's unity, holiness, immensity, eternality, and truthfulness.

---

[1] For more on the scriptural foundation of these four adjectives, see Richard D. Phillips, Philip G. Ryken, Mark E. Dever, *The Church: One, Holy, Catholic and Apostolic* (Phillipsburg: P&R, 2004). Cf. J. C. Ryle, *Knots Untied*, 10th ed. (London, 1885), 217–18; R. B. Kuiper, *The Glorious Body of Christ* (Carlisle, PA: Banner of Truth, 1967), 41–72; Louis Berkhof, *Systematic Theology*, 4th ed. (Grand Rapids: Eerdmans, 1941), 572–76. A number of ecclesiologies have been structured following these four characteristics of the church; e.g., G. C. Berkouwer, *The Church*, transl. James E. Davison (Grand Rapids: Eerdmans, 1976); Gabriel Fackre, *The Church: Signs of the Spirit and Signs of the Time* (Grand Rapids: Eerdmans, 2007); and partially, Michael Horton, *People and Place: A Covenant Ecclesiology* (Louisville: Westminster/John Knox, 2008). In his first chapter Berkouwer discussed the relation of the four classic attributes with the Reformers' marks of a true church, especially pp. 7–17.

One

The church is one and is to be one because God is one. Christians have always been characterized by their unity (Acts 4:32). The unity of Christians in the church is to be a property of the church, and a sign for the world reflecting the unity of God himself. Thus, divisions and quarrels are a peculiarly serious scandal. Paul wrote to the Ephesians, "There is one body and one Spirit—just as you were called to one hope when you were called—one Lord, one faith, one baptism; one God and Father of all, who is over all and through all and in all" (Eph 4:4–6). In 1 Corinthians 1, Paul argued for the unity of the Christians based on their unity in Christ. In Romans 12 and 1 Corinthians 12, Paul taught there is one body. And in Gal 3:27–28, Paul said that Christians are all one in Christ, regardless of ethnicity. He also called the Philippian church to unity (Phil 2:2). Paul's teaching reflects Christ's own teaching that there is one flock (John 10:16). Therefore Christ prayed in John 17:21 for his followers to be one.

The church is one, though divided.[2] This unity is not visible at the organizational level; it is a spiritual reality, consisting in the fellowship of all true believers sharing in the Holy Spirit. It becomes visible when believers share the same baptism, partake of the same supper, and look forward to sharing one heavenly city. The church on earth experiences this unity only as its members are united in God's truth as it is revealed in Scripture.

Holy

The church is holy and is to be holy because God is holy.[3] The holiness of the church describes God's declaration concerning his people as well as the Spirit's progressive work. After all, the church is the dwelling place of the Holy Spirit, and it is composed of saints set apart for God's special use (see 1 Cor 1:2). So the church's holiness is fundamentally Christ's holiness. It possesses it by the declaration of God.

---

[2] See Hans Kung, *The Church*, 320.
[3] Lev 11:44–45; 19:2; 20:7; 1 Pet 1:14–16.

At the same time, Christ's holiness will be reflected in the church's holiness.[4] Christ "loved the church and gave himself up for her to make her holy, cleansing her by the washing with water through the word, and to present her to himself as a radiant church, without stain or wrinkle or any other blemish, but holy and blameless" (Eph 5:25–27). In this present age the church will never attain ethical holiness perfectly. "The Lord is daily at work in smoothing out wrinkles and cleansing spots. From this it follows that the church's holiness is not yet complete. The church is holy, then, in the sense that it is daily advancing and is not yet perfect."[5]

But the holy status the church possesses by virtue of God's declaratory act also separates the church from the world for God's service. Hence, both the Old and New Testaments emphasize the importance of holiness among the people of God so that they might accomplish that service to which they are called.[6] Certainly a church which resigns itself to evil fails dismally. This holiness of status is a being-set-apart, not a being-cut-off, which results in holiness of action in the world.

Universal

The church is universal and is to be universal because God is the "Lord of all the earth"[7] and "King of the ages."[8] The church is universal in that it stretches across space and time. Universality alone among these four attributes is not actually found in the New Testament. Rather this description developed from later reflection upon the true church. "Catholic" is the older English word used to describe this attribute. But because of that word's association with the Church of Rome, "universality" provides a better translation of the Greek word *katholicain* originally used in the creeds.

---

[4] Rom 6:14; Phil 3:8–9.
[5] John Calvin, *Institutes of the Christian Religion*, in *Library of Christian Classics*, vol. xx, ed. John T. McNeill, trans. Ford Lewis Battles (Philadelphia: Westminster, 1960), IV.i.17.
[6] Deut 14:2; 1 Cor 5–6; 2 Cor 6:14–7:1.
[7] Josh 3:11,13; Ps 97:5; Mic 4:13; Zech 4:14; cf. Jer 23:24.
[8] Rev 15:3.

Universality is not the domain of any one group of true Christians. In Ignatius of Antioch's letter to the Smyrneans in the early second century AD, he wrote that "where Jesus Christ is there is the universal church" (*Smyrn.* 8.2). From the third century AD, the word came to be used synonymously with "orthodox," as opposed to "heretical," "schismatic," and "innovative."[9]

While every true local church is part of this universal church and is an entire church itself, no local church can be said to constitute the entire universal church. Therefore, Christians must exercise care in their assumptions about the correctness of doctrines or practices that may, in fact, be peculiar to their own time or place. Ever since the initial inclusion of Gentiles into the first-century church, the church has obeyed Christ's mandate to spread his gospel to all nations, so that the church will finally be composed of people from all nations. "You are worthy to take the scroll and to open its seals, because you were slain, and with your blood you purchased men for God from every tribe and language and people and nation" (Rev 5:9). The continuity of the church across space and time prevents the church from being held captive to any one segment of it. The church, in both its local and universal manifestations, belongs to Christ and Christ alone.

Apostolic

The church is apostolic and is to be apostolic because it is founded on and is faithful to the Word of God given through the apostles. Early in Jesus' public ministry, Jesus "called his disciples to him and chose twelve of them, whom he also designated apostles" (Luke 6:13). Toward the end of his ministry, Jesus then prayed "for those who will believe in me through their [the apostles'] message" (John 17:20).

---

[9] For example, see Clement of Alexandria in Henry Bettenson, ed., *The Early Christian Fathers: A Selection from the Writings of the Fathers from St. Clement to St. Athanasius* (New York: Oxford University Press, 1956), 247; for further discussion see Mark Dever, "A Catholic Church: Galatians 3:26–29," in Richard D. Phillips, Philip G. Ryken, and Mark Dever, eds., *The Church: One, Holy , Catholic, and Apostolic* (Phillipsburg, NJ: P&R, 2004), 71–72.

From the apostles until the present day, the gospel which they preached has been handed down. There has been a succession of apostolic teaching based on the Word of God. Paul tells the Ephesian Christians that they had been "built on the foundation of the apostles and prophets, with Christ Jesus himself as the chief cornerstone" (Eph 2:20). The succession which followed the setting of this foundation may not always have involved a person-to-person transmission, but there has been a succession of faithful teaching of the truth. Writing to the Galatians, Paul stressed that their allegiance to the gospel message he had already given them superseded any allegiance to him personally (see Gal 1:6–9).

What does that mean for today since the apostles are long gone? Some Protestants have been hesitant to affirm this attribute because the Roman Catholic Church has interpreted it as being tied to the authority of the bishop of Rome. Yet the apostles' teaching rather than their persons are the focus of this attribute. Edmund Clowney put it succinctly: "To compromise the authority of Scripture is to destroy the apostolic foundation of the church."[10] The physical continuity of a line of pastor-elders back to Christ's apostles is insignificant compared to the continuity between the teaching in churches today and the teaching of the apostles.[11] Only with the apostles' teaching is the church "the pillar and foundation of the truth," as Paul described it to Timothy (1 Tim 3:15).

These four attributes have long been used to express the Bible's teaching about the church. They are the church's gifts and tasks. One theologian summarized:

> The church is already one, but it must become more visibly one ... in faith and practice. The church is already holy in its source and foundation, but it must strive to produce fruits of holiness in its sojourn in the world. The church is already catholic, but it must

---

[10] Clowney, *The Church*, 76.
[11] Robert Reymond commented on this succinctly: "Just as the true seed of Abraham are those who walk in the faith of Abraham, irrespective of lineal descent, so also the apostolic church is one which walks in the faith of the apostles, irrespective of the issue of 'unbroken succession'" (*New Systematic Theology*, 844).

seek a fuller measure of catholicity by assimilating the valid protests against church abuse . . . into its own life. The church is already apostolic, but it must become more consciously apostolic by allowing the gospel to reform and sometimes even overturn its time-honored rites and interpretations.[12]

---

[12] Donald Bloesch, *The Church* (Downers Grove: IVP, 2002), 103.

3

The Marks of the Church

Over the centuries the four attributes of the church have been joined and often replaced by two marks that define a local church.[1] These two marks are the right preaching of the Word of God and the right administration of baptism and the Lord's Supper.[2] In fact, a biblical ecclesiology can largely be organized and presented under these two marks since in them both the creation and the preservation of the church are accomplished. The first mark is the fountain of God's truth that gives life to his people, and the second is the lovely vessel to contain and display this glorious work. The church is generated by the right preaching of the Word. The church is distinguished and contained by the right administration of baptism and the Lord's Supper. It should also be noted that this latter mark presumes and implies the practice of church discipline. The rest of this section is

---

[1] For an interesting comparison of the function of the classic four attributes (unity, holiness, universality, apostolicity) and the two marks of a true church, see Kung, *The Church*, 267–69.

[2] The language of "marks" is the classic word used in English to consider those characteristics that distinguish a true church from a false church. I have used the word "marks" in another, more popular way in my books *Nine Marks of a Healthy Church*, rev. ed. (Wheaton, IL: Crossway, 2004) and *What Is a Healthy Church?* (Wheaton, IL: Crossway, 2007). In these books "marks" refers to characteristics of a church, some of which are essential to its being a true church, others of which distinguish between true churches that are more healthy and those that are unhealthy. For more on this, see the introduction to *9 Marks of a Healthy Church*.

devoted to an investigation of the Bible's teaching on the church organized under these two heads: first, the right preaching of the Word; second, the right administration of the ordinances. Several implications of the right administration of the ordinances are also considered, including membership, polity, discipline, and the purpose of the church.

Right Preaching as a Mark of a True Church

Right Preaching of the Word

God's people in Scripture are created by God's revelation of himself. His Spirit accompanies his Word and brings life.

The theme of "life through the Word" is clear in both the Old and New Testaments. In the Old Testament, God created life in Genesis 1 by his breath. God spoke and the world and all living beings were created. In Gen 1:30, the living creatures are described as having the "breath of life"[3] in them. So in Gen 2:7, God breathed this same breath of life into those creatures made specially in his image—men and women.

After the first man and woman fell away from God by rebelling against him, God sustained them and their descendants by his word—a word of promise given to them in Gen 3:15. Again in Gen 12:1–3, his word called Abram from Ur of the Chaldees to become the progenitor of God's people. In Exod 3:4, God called on Moses with his word to bring his people out of Egypt. In Exodus 20, God gave his people his 10 "words," and throughout the Pentateuch, God's Word is the shaping influence on his people. Throughout the Old Testament, God ministered to his people by his word. He created them and recreated them through the priests' teaching of the law and the prophets' inspired guidance.

Ezekiel 37 presents a dramatic picture of recreation in particular. The people of Israel were in exile, depicted as an army so devastated only their bones remained. God commanded the prophet Ezekiel to preach to these bones. As Ezekiel did, the Spirit of God accompanied Ezekiel's words, and the bones were brought to life:

---

[3] נֶפֶשׁ חַיָּה.

> And as I was prophesying, there was a noise, a rat-
> tling sound, and the bones came together, bone to
> bone. I looked, and tendons and flesh appeared on
> them and skin covered them, but there was no breath
> in them. Then he said to me, "Prophesy to the breath;
> prophesy, son of man, and say to it, 'This is what the
> Sovereign Lᴏʀᴅ says: Come from the four winds, O
> breath, and breathe into these slain, that they may
> live.'" So I prophesied as he commanded me, and
> breath entered them; they came to life and stood up
> on their feet—a vast army. (vv. 7–10)

The consistent message of Scripture is that God created his
people and brings them to life through his word.

Moving to the New Testament, God's word again plays
the central role as the bringer of life. So the eternal Word of
God, the Son of God, became incarnate for the salvation of
God's people (John 1:14). Jesus came to preach God's word,
to uniquely embody it, as well as to accomplish God's will
through his perfect life, atoning death, and triumphant resurrection. He founded his church and taught his followers
to go into all nations, preaching the message of reconcilia-
tion to God through faith in him (Matt 28:18–20). Therefore,
Paul wrote that "faith comes from hearing the message, and
the message is heard through the word of Christ" (Rom
10:17).

The Framework of Right Preaching: Biblical Theology

The right preaching of the word of God that created the
church is not only the word from God; it is also the word
about God. As the call to hear (the Shema) puts it, "Hear,
O Israel: The Lᴏʀᴅ our God, the Lᴏʀᴅ is one" (Deut 6:4).
Immediately following this statement about God is the command indicating the response required of God's people: "Love
the Lᴏʀᴅ your God with all your heart and with all your soul
and with all your strength" (Deut 6:5). When asked which
command was the most important, Jesus pointed to this one
(Matt 22:37). Not only is it echoed throughout the Old and

New Testaments,[4] it summarizes the whole law and fundamentally marks out the identity of those who belong to God.
When God's people hear about God and what he requires,
they *will* respond.

In that sense a right understanding of God provides the
right framework for right preaching. Everything a preacher
says must be placed within and shaped by the grid of biblical theology that teaches both preacher and congregation
about God and what he requires of humanity. After all, a
right understanding of God can be the only true foundation
for the church.

According to the Bible, the church has as its Creator and
Lord, and as its center, the God of the Bible. This God is creating, holy, faithful, loving, and sovereign. The God of the
Bible is recognized as the great Initiator. This means that
he is the Creator of the world and the Giver of everything. It
also means he is the Author of the church's salvation (Heb
2:10). The salvation offered inside the church through the
preached word is not originally from the church. The church
merely acts as the means, or the instrument, through which
the great creating and electing God calls his people to himself. God's people exist because of his pleasure (Eph 1:9–13).

The God of the Bible is also the holy God. Holiness is an
attribute of God's own character, his nature, and the nature
of all of his works. Of course, God's holiness is a problem for
sinful people because it separates all humans from God. Yet
it characterizes God's unique self and his unique loveliness.
Without this holiness—his utter moral purity—God would
not be God. And he has created a people who are called to
reflect his holy character through lives marked by holiness
(Lev 11:44–45; 19:2; 20:7; 1 Pet 1:16).

The God of the Bible is a faithful God. He keeps his promises. When he promises to make a people his own, they will
be made his own. The Old and New Testaments are a grand
and sometimes elaborate account of God's making promises
to his people and then keeping them. From the promise to
forgive (Exod 34:6–7) to the promise to provide a prophet

---

[4] E.g., 2 Chr 15:12; Isa 44:6–8; John 17:3; 1 Cor 8:5–6; Jas 2:19.

like Moses (Deut 18:15–19), God's Old Testament promises were fulfilled to his people in the New Testament through the person and work of Jesus Christ. Jesus is the ransom and the lamb, the prophet and the priest, the second Adam and the faithful Son. In all these ways God's faithfulness makes a people for himself.

The God of the Bible is a loving God. But his love can be understood maximally only when counterpoised to his holiness because his love provides what his holiness requires. Apart from God's holiness the church *need* not exist. That is, if God is not set apart, his people need not be set apart. But apart from God's love the church *would* not exist. Only God himself can set his people apart, and why would God set them apart unless he loved them? So the whole message God brings to his people can be summarized as judgment and grace, holiness and mercy, human sin and divine forgiveness through Christ. "For God so loved the world that he gave his one and only Son, that whoever believes in him shall not perish but have eternal life" (John 3:16).

And the God of the Bible is a sovereign God. So Jesus taught his disciples to pray by approaching God as the sovereign king: "Your kingdom come, your will be done on earth as it is in heaven" (Matt 6:10). The God who is the Creator and Lord of the church is also the Creator and Lord of all that has been made. His rule will be acknowledged by all at the end—in one way or another. Some will greet his coming with shouts of joy and gladness, others with fists and teeth clenched in resentment. But all will acknowledge he is sovereign. In that sense the church is an in-breaking of his rule into this present age, a foretaste of heaven.

This is the God his people are commanded to love. All other gods are a creation of the human mind and will share in the vanishing fate of every other illusion. The God of the Bible must be the foundation and framework of all teaching and preaching in the church.

The Center of Right Teaching: The Gospel

If a right theology of God provides the framework, or grid, for right teaching, then a focus on the gospel provides the center, or point, of right teaching. As we have seen, false teaching about God separates God's people from him and builds a community around a being who does not exist. Furthermore, if the god preached is not offended by sin and does not judge sinners, then the gospel itself is short-circuited. People are lied to in a manner which imperils their salvation. The right teaching of the true church, therefore, centers itself upon a right understanding of the gospel.

Right teaching about the gospel, in turn, requires a right understanding not only about God but also about humanity. If a church's teaching depicts people as merely spiritually sick, not spiritually dead, the gospel has been distorted. If congregants are regarded as consumers rightly expectant of a spiritual upgrade, not as rebels before a holy judge, then the gospel has probably been forgotten. Such churches build community around something other than the gospel. Any unity they experience is a unity based on a false message.

Right teaching about the gospel also centers the church on Christ's work of atonement and not only on his teaching or life example. The true church is cruciform, not necessarily in its architecture but in its teaching. Jesus' life does provide an example for Christian living. So say both Christ and the apostles (Matt 10:25; Mark 8:34; 1 Pet 2:21). But what sets Christian teaching apart from every other major religion is that its head acts as both example and Redeemer. Christ came not only to preach but also to be a ransom for his people (Mark 10:45). Thus when the church gathers, it gathers not simply as an instructed or edified people but as a ransomed and saved people.

Finally, right teaching about the gospel centers the church not on human actions but on receiving by faith and repentance the rewards of God's actions in Christ. Paul wrote to the Corinthians, "God made him [Christ] who had no sin to be sin for us, so that in him we might become the righteousness of God" (2 Cor 5:21). Sinful humanity has earned God's judgment. But through repentance and faith, sinners are made God's own people. Churches must not err by neglecting either repentance or faith. Without the former, a mental-assent-only faith follows, which is dead (see

Jas 2:17,26). Without the latter, faith and reliance on Christ vanish behind demands of obedience to the law (see Romans 2–3). A gospel-centered church teaches the need to both turn from sin and turn to Christ. By itself a searching exposition on human sin is not enough. By itself the proclamation of God's love in Christ's atoning death is not enough. Both are necessary. A cross not taken up by repentance or affirmed by faith is a cross that does not save. The right preaching of the Word of God is central to the church and is the basis and core of it.

Right Administration of the Ordinances

Right Administration of the Ordinances as a Mark of a True Church

Jesus Christ gave two visible signs of his special presence to his people. These signs are baptism and the Lord's Supper. Sometimes they are called "ordinances," emphasizing the fact that they were ordained by Christ. Other times they are called "sacraments."[5] Some evangelicals are hesitant to use the latter term because it suggests that the signs are effective apart from a believer's faith.[6] Therefore, the term *ordinances* is used in this chapter except when describing positions in which the original source used *sacrament*.

Christ himself ordained these practices both by example and by command. He was baptized by John the Baptist, and he commanded his disciples to make disciples in all nations and baptize them.[7] Based on Acts and the letters, it seems this was the universal practice of New Testament Christians. Christ also established the Supper and commanded his

---

[5] The earliest usage extant of the term *sacramentum* to describe both baptism and the Lord's Supper is by Tertullian. He seems to have used this to mean not so much a "mystery" (see Jerome's Vulgate translation of Eph 1:9; 3:3; 5:32) as an "oath," like one a soldier would swear in being initiated into service. Thanks to Gordon Hugenberger for sharing some of his research on this point. Louis Berkhof defined a sacrament as an ordinance (*Systematic Theology*, 617).

[6] "Let it be regarded as a settled principle that the sacraments have the same office as the Word of God: to offer and set forth Christ to us, and in him the treasures of heavenly grace. But they avail and profit nothing unless received in faith" (Calvin, *Institutes*, IV.xiv.17).

[7] Matt 3:15–16; Mark 1:9; Luke 3:21; John 1:29–34; Matt 28:19.

disciples to "do this in remembrance of" him.[8] From the rest
of the New Testament, it seems clear that Christians regularly partook of what Paul called "the Lord's Supper" (1 Cor
11:20).[9]

When churches practice baptism and the Lord's Supper,
they obey Christ's teaching and example. In so doing, they
portray Christ's death and resurrection, the testimony of
every believer's own spiritual birth, as well as the church's
collective hope for the final resurrection and reunion with
the Lord. These two practices, in short, proclaim the gospel.
Thus, even congregations that have long forsaken biblical
doctrine regarding regeneration, Christ's substitutionary
death, or the hope of heaven, still proclaim these truths in
their liturgies as they reenact these signs. The new birth
may be ignored, but baptism portrays it. Christ's atonement
may be denied in the sermon, but the Supper proclaims it.[10]
In such cases tradition at the table speaks more truth than
the preaching from the pulpit. Practicing baptism and the
Lord's Supper demonstrates obedience to Christ, and they
are intended to complement by visible sign and symbol the
audible preaching of the gospel.

Conversely, a church fails to obey Christ's command
when it neglects either of these two signs.[11] Such failure removes that church from a submission to the larger
teaching of Scripture. And it separates a congregation from
the apostolic and universal practice of Christ's followers.
Scripture acts as a counterweight against anyone—whether
a congregation or a person—who decides to be a Christian
and yet neglects baptism or the Lord's Supper. This neglect,
or denial, separates the person from those who truly follow Christ. While neither baptism nor the Lord's Supper is
salvific, a deliberate neglect of either puts a question mark

---

[8] Matt 26:17–30; Mark 14:12–26; Luke 22:7–20; 1 Cor 11:17–34.
[9] κυριακὸν δεῖπνον.
[10] "For whenever you eat this bread and drink this cup, you proclaim the Lord's death until he comes" (1 Cor 11:26).
[11] The organized bodies of confessing followers of Christ which deliberately reject these practices are the Quakers and the Salvation Army. Many contemporary evan-gelical congregations could also be said to neglect baptism or the Lord's Supper in practice if they are evaluated by either frequency or understanding.

on any profession of faith. In this sense baptism and the Lord's Supper act as the marks of a true church. They are the outward signs, or visible boundaries, which distinguish a particular people from the world. Yet matching that outward message is an inward message. The ordinances remind Christians of the fellowship they enjoy with God and one another.

Some have taught that other ordinances or sacraments mark the true church. The Roman Catholic Church teaches that confirmation, confession (penance), ordination, marriage, and extreme unction (last rites) are also sacraments.[12] Yet due to the Roman Catholic Church's teaching about the authority of the church and the role of tradition, they need not convincingly maintain that these are all ordained of Christ during the time of his earthly ministry.[13] In the early sixteenth century, however, the Protestant reformers recognized the Bible alone as authoritative for establishing church practice, resulting in the claim that only baptism and the Lord's Supper had sufficient warrant to be regarded as sacraments which were binding on churches.[14] Among some Baptists and other Protestant groups, foot-washing has been treated as a church ordinance, following Christ's example and words in John 13:14. Yet neither churches in the New Testament nor in the immediate subapostolic

---

[12] The Council of Trent finally determined seven as the number of sacraments faithful Roman Catholics should accept. The other five, with their biblical bases are confirmation (Acts 8:17; 14:22; 19:6; Heb 6:2), confession (Jas 5:16), ordination (1 Tim 4:14; 2 Tim 1:6), marriage (Eph 5:32), and extreme unction (Jas 5:14). See paragraph 1113 in *Catechism of the Catholic Church*, in *Libreria Editrice Vaticana* (Liguori: Liguori Publications, 1994). At some length Calvin rejected these five additional practices as sacraments (*Institutes*, IV.xix). Berkouwer concluded his consideration of the five "extra" Roman Catholic sacraments by gently stating that "this brief review of the five special sacraments makes it clear that Roman Catholic theology fixes the number of sacraments on the basis of its view that they constitute a series of supernatural acts that infuse supernatural grace into all of life from beginning to end, rather than upon an indubitable foundation of biblical exegesis" (G. C. Berkouwer, *The Sacraments*, trans. Hugo Bekker [Grand Rapids: Eerdmans, 1969], 36).

[13] Modern Roman Catholic theology has spoken of the entire church as being a sacrament. E.g., "the Church, in Christ, is in the nature of sacrament—a sign and instrument, that is, of communion with God and of unity among all men" ("Dogmatic Constitution of the Church" in *Vatican Council II*, Austin Flannery ed. [Northport, NY: Costello Pub. Co., 1975], 350).

[14] E.g., Article 26 of the 39 Articles of Religion of the Church of England.

period give evidence of having understood foot-washing in
this way.[15] The words of Christ in John 13:14 seem rather
to teach humility. Foot-washing is an action illustrating a
command ("love one another") rather than a promise, as
both baptism and the Lord's Supper are.[16]

Baptism. Though Paul spoke of "one baptism" shared
by all Christians (Eph 4:5), Scripture surely recounts more
baptisms than one.[17] The Christian church is commanded
to practice baptism by immersing a person in water who
both professes and evidences conversion. This baptism is
performed in obedience to Christ as a confession of sin, a
profession of faith in Christ, and a display of hope in the
resurrection of the body. It is performed only once. The
proper mode, subjects, and significance of baptism are now
considered.

Proper Mode. Baptism is generally understood to have
been practiced by immersion in the New Testament church.[18]
Eastern Orthodox Churches have always understood *bap-
tizein*[19] to mean "to immerse" and therefore have always
practiced baptism by immersion. The Roman Catholic
Church and most Protestant churches admit the antiquity
of immersion, but they deny that a particular mode is essential for valid baptism.[20] While it is difficult to maintain that

---

[15] See John L. Dagg, *Treatise on Church Order* (1858; repr., Harrisonburg: Gano
Books, 1982), 226–31. Dagg laid out five arguments against taking the command
to wash one another's feet as a lasting ordinance for the church.

[16] The author is indebted to Ligon Duncan for this careful and helpful distinction.

[17] The Old Testament contains many ceremonial washings (see Heb 9:10). Paul
used the image of baptism to explain the people of Israel's submersion into the
law of God (1 Cor 10:1–2). John the Baptist distinguished his baptism from Jesus'
(John 1:24–27,33; cf. Luke 3:3). Paul also explained the difference in Ephesus (Acts
19:1–6). Jesus taught that his disciples would be baptized by the Holy Spirit (Acts
1:5). Jesus referred to his own death metaphorically as a baptism (Luke 12:50). And
among the Corinthian Christians there was even a practice of baptism for the dead
(1 Cor 15:29). For more on the historical background of baptism in the first century, see George R. Beasley-Murray, *Baptism in the New Testament* (Grand Rapids:
Eerdmans, 1962), 1–92.

[18] See F. M. Buhler, *Baptism, Three Aspects: Archaeological, Historical, Biblical,*
trans. W. P. Bauman (Dundas, Ontario, Canada: Joshua Press, 2004).

[19] βαπτίζειν.

[20] Thomas Aquinas wrote: "In the sacrament of Baptism water is put to the use of
a washing of the body, whereby to signify the inward washing away of sins. Now
washing may be done with water not only by immersion, but also by sprinkling
or pouring. And, therefore, although it is safer to baptize by immersion, because
this is the more ordinary fashion, yet Baptism can be conferred by sprinkling or

baptizo[21] could only mean "immerse" in the New Testament era,[22] immersion does seem both to be the most straightforward meaning of the word itself (thus the unbroken practice of immersion among Greek-speaking churches) and to best fit the uses of the word in the New Testament.[23] As Millard

---

also by pouring, according to Ezekiel 36:25: 'I will pour upon you clean water.' . . . And this especially in cases of urgency: either because there is a great number to be baptized, as was clearly the case in Acts 2 and 4, where we read that on one day three thousand believed, and on another five thousand: or through there being but a small supply of water, or through feebleness of the minister, who cannot hold up the candidate for Baptism; or through feebleness of the candidate, whose life might be endangered by immersion. We must therefore conclude that immersion is not necessary for Baptism," *Summa Theologica* (CD-ROM: AGES Software, 1997) Question 66, Answer 7. John Calvin recognized the antiquity of immersion but not its necessity for valid baptism: "Whether the person being baptized should be wholly immersed, and whether thrice or once, whether he should only be sprinkled with poured water—these details are of no importance, but ought to be optional to churches according to diversity of countries. Yet the word 'baptize' means to immerse, and it is clear that the rite of immersion was observed in the ancient church" (*Institutes*, IV.xv.19). For a typical representative Lutheran consideration of the issue, see David P. Scaer, *Baptism* (St. Louis: The Luther Academy, 1999), 91–101.

[21] βαπτίζω.

[22] E.g., in chap. 7 of *The Didache* (dating most likely from the late first or early second century), we read: "Now concerning baptism (βαπτίσματος), baptize as follows: after you have reviewed all these things, baptize 'in the name of the Father and of the Son and of the Holy Spirit' in running (ζῶτι) water. But if you have no running water, then baptize in some other water; and if you are not able to baptize in cold water, then do so in warm. But if you have neither then pour (ἐκχεον) water on the head three times 'in the name of the Father and Son and Holy Spirit,'" (*The Didache*, in *The Apostolic Fathers*, 2nd ed., trans. J. B. Lightfoot and J. R. Harmer [1891; repr. Grand Rapids: Baker, 1992], 258–59. *The Didache* is, of course, not Scripture and is in no way normative for the practice of Christians today. But it is lexically significant that, in this document, first-/ (or early second-/) century Greek-speaking Christians could refer to ἐκχεον as a βαπτίσματος (baptism).

[23] One of the most recent defenses of pouring as baptism argues that Rom 6:3–6; Heb 9:10–19; Titus 3:5–6; and Ezek 36:25–27 demonstrate that baptism symbolizes the Holy Spirit's being poured out in connection with the Christian's being washed from sins as part of union with Christ, none of which require immersion, and any of which may have more normally been signified by pouring (see Joseph Pipa, "The Mode of Baptism," in *The Case for Covenantal Infant Baptism*, ed. Gregg Strawbridge [Phillipsburg: P&R, 2003], 112–26). Overarguing for immersion makes for arguments like Pipa's, which are perhaps overarguings in the opposite direction (i.e., for pouring or sprinkling). It is not disputed that βαπτίζειν means "to wash" fully and completely, at least when used for symbolic purposes. For a recent defense of immersion, see Tom Wells, *Does Baptism Mean Immersion?* (Laurel, MS: Audubon Press, 2000); cf. Wayne Grudem, *Systematic Theology* (Grand Rapids: IVP, 1994), 967–68. For an example of a historical defense of immersion, see John Gill, *A Body of Doctrinal and Practical Divinity*, new edition (London: Mathews & Leigh Co., 1839), 909–14. The nineteenth-century denominational debates had thousands of pages published investigating every side of this controversy; e.g., John L. Dagg, *Church Order*, 21–65.

Erickson wrote, "It is not possible to resolve the issue of
the proper mode of baptism on the basis of linguistic data
alone. . . . While [immersion] may not be the only valid
form of baptism, it is the form that most fully preserves and
accomplishes the meaning of baptism."[24]

Proper Subjects. As an adult Jesus Christ was himself a
proper subject of baptism. Though circumcised as a descen-
dant of Abraham, Jesus said the purpose of his baptism was
"to fulfill all righteousness" (Matt 3:15). By accepting John's
baptism, Jesus indicated his acceptance of the will and plan
of the Father to begin his public ministry.

According to the Scriptures, Christian baptism is exclusively meant for those who believe in Christ and follow him.
Four reasons support this statement. First, those who evangelize are commanded to baptize only those who repent and
believe (Matt 28:18–20; cf. John 4:1–2). Second, the only
clearly recorded subjects of baptism in the book of Acts are
individuals who have repented and believed (see Acts 2:37–41;
8:12–13,36–38; 9:18; 10:47–48; 16:15,33; 18:8; 19:5). Third,
Paul's letters demonstrate the twin assumptions that those
who have believed have been baptized and that those who
have been baptized believe (see Rom 6:1–5; Gal 3:26–27; Col
2:11–12). Finally, Peter associated baptism with salvation not
as a cause of salvation but as a roughly contemporary occur-
rence (Acts 2:38; 1 Pet 3:21). Through direct command,
examples of obedience, Paul's assumptions, and Peter's associations, the Scriptures teach that baptism is for believers.

Baptism functions as both a confession of sin and a profession of faith for the believer. Faith is professed in Christ
and the objective realities of Christ's death, the gift of the
Spirit, and the final resurrection—all of which are depicted
in baptism. Furthermore, it testifies to the subjective experiences of confession and forgiveness, spiritual regeneration,

---

[24] Millard Erickson, *Christian Theology*, 1113–14; cf. Robert Saucy's comment:
"It would seem that the basic significance of baptism, namely, identification with
Christ and his saving work, might, if necessary, be signified through a mode other
than immersion, even as the early church provided. The evidence points, however,
to immersion as the standard practice of the New Testament church and the mode
which most fully signifies Christian salvation" (*The Church in God's Program*
[Chicago: Moody, 1972], 212–13).

and the newly discovered resurrection hope. Baptism portrays the Christian's union with Christ and therefore with other Christians and the church (see Rom 6:1–14).

Water baptism does not create the reality of saving grace or faith in the one being baptized.[25] Rather, it testifies to the presence of such grace and faith.[26] Justification, regeneration, and fellowship with Christ and his people are all received through the word of the gospel. But, as Herman Bavinck put it, "These benefits are further signified and sealed to them in baptism."[27] Peter exhorted each of his hearers to "repent and be baptized . . . in the name of Jesus Christ for the forgiveness of your sins" (Acts 2:38).[28] Baptism does not cause sins to be forgiven. Rather, faith apprehends the forgiveness of sins and responds to the commands for repentance and obedience in baptism. In his first letter Peter mentioned the waters of the flood in Noah's day: "This water symbolizes baptism that now saves you also—not the removal of dirt from the body but the pledge of a good conscience toward God. It saves you by the resurrection of Jesus Christ, who has gone into heaven and is at God's right hand" (1 Pet 3:21–22). Christians have a good conscience through God's grace by the resurrection of Jesus Christ. This salvation is not created but is symbolized by baptism. Berkhof said, "It is a seal, not merely of an offered, but of an offered and accepted, that is, of a concluded covenant."[29] And as Calvin explained, "It is the mark by which we publicly profess that we wish to be reckoned God's people."[30]

Though everyone has always agreed that the Bible teaches believers should be baptized, the practice of baptizing infants has long been a matter of debate. Some have suggested that infants should be baptized because baptism itself

---

[25] Were baptism essential for salvation, Paul could never have said that "Christ did not send me to baptize, but to preach the gospel" (1 Cor 1:17).

[26] Such testimony should occur in the context of a believing community, whose responsibility it is to test the credibility of the profession.

[27] Herman Bavinck, *Reformed Dogmatics: Holy Spirit, Church and New Creation*, vol. 4 (Grand Rapids: Baker Academic, 2008), 521.

[28] ἐπὶ τῷ ὀνόματι Ἰησοῦ Χριστοῦ εἰς ἄφεσιν τῶν ἁμαρτιῶν ὑμῶν.

[29] Berkhof, *Systematic Theology*, 632; cf. his comments on proper recipients of the Lord's Supper on p. 657.

[30] Calvin, *Institutes*, IV.xv.13.

is the instrument God's Spirit uses to regenerate the infant
(see Acts 2:38; 22:16; 1 Pet 3:21). But as stated above, the
New Testament in no way teaches that baptism is salvific.
Others have suggested that an infant born into a Christian
family belongs to Abraham's seed and that baptism declares
the infant to be a recipient of the promises God made to his
people through Abraham (see Gen 12:7; 17:7; Acts 7:5; Gal
3:16). Christian baptism in the New Testament is treated as
parallel to Old Testament circumcision.[31] But the Scriptures
do not clearly support this latter view either. Not only is baptism expressly said to be for those who believe, as considered
above, but the promises to Abraham's seed are explicitly fulfilled in Christ (see Gal 3:16).

Furthermore, baptism with water is expressly said in the
New Testament not to be analogous to physical circumcision
but to circumcision of the heart (see Col 2:11–12). Both the
Abrahamic covenant and the new covenant are covenants of
grace. Yet God promised the Israelites that a change would
occur in the spiritual solidarity of the physical family in the
coming new covenant.[32] Jeremiah wrote that "everyone will
die for his own sin" (Jer 31:30). In the new covenant,

> The covenantees are not those who are *born* into the
> covenant, those whose father and mother have the
> law "written upon their hearts," but those who *them-*
> *selves* have had this experience, having been born
> again by the Spirit of God. This subjective, inward,
> existential, experiential, spiritual change is the hall-
> mark of the new covenant.[33]

---

[31] For a defense of infant baptism from a Lutheran perspective, see A. Andrew Das,
Baptized into God's Family: The Doctrine of Infant Baptism for Today, 2nd ed.
(Milwaukee: Northwestern Publishing House, 2008).

[32] Stephen J. Wellum offered an especially helpful discussion of continuity and
discontinuity between the old and new covenant with respect to baptism. He recognized the strengths of the traditional argument from covenant theology for infant
baptism but also observed how covenant theologians can flatten the biblical text in
order to make their theological assertions. See his "Baptism and the Relationship
Between the Covenants," in *Believer's Baptism: Sign of the New Covenant in
Christ,* ed. Thomas R. Schreiner and Shawn D. Wright (Nashville: B&H Academic,
2006), 97–161.

[33] Paul K. Jewett, *Infant Baptism and the Covenant of Grace* (Grand Rapids:
Eerdmans, 1978), 228; cf. Fred Malone, *The Baptism of Disciples Alone:*

While the topics of both children and baptism occur in the New Testament, the two never occur together in either explicit teaching or example. Whether construed as a matter of salvific cause or covenantal promise, any teaching which separates baptism from saving belief misrepresents Scripture and potentially confuses the gospel itself.[34]

While Scripture clearly reserves baptism for believers, it does not directly address the age at which believers should be baptized. Nor does the command to baptize forbid raising questions about the appropriateness of a baptismal candidate's maturity. The fact that believers are commanded to be baptized does not give a church license to baptize indiscriminately, especially where maturity-of-life issues make it difficult to assess the credibility of a profession of faith. New Testament baptisms largely appear to have occurred shortly after conversion, but every specific individual mentioned is an adult coming from a non-Christian context, two factors which make the church's job of attesting to the credibility of a profession of faith simple and straightforward.

As a matter of Christian wisdom and prudence, therefore, the normal age of baptism should be when the credibility of one's conversion becomes naturally discernable and evident to the church community. A legitimate secondary concern is the effect of the child's baptism on other families in the church. The least spiritually discerning parents— with the best intentions—have too often brought pressure on their compliant children to be baptized. Such children have thereby been wrongly assured of their salvation and have been further hardened to hearing the gospel later in life. Tragically, the hope they most need may be hidden by the act meant to display it.

The Bible's teaching on baptism is clear in institution, command, and fulfillment. People enter the new covenant by God's grace, and the means God has graciously chosen

---

A Covenantal Argument for Credobaptism Versus Paedobaptism (Cape Coral, FL: Founders, 2003).

[34] David Wright (*What Has Infant Baptism Done to Baptism?* [Carlisle, UK: Paternoster, 2005]), himself a paedo-baptist, made an interesting contribution to this discussion by criticizing the effects of widespread infant baptism.

to use is faith. Faith is not caused or created by baptism. Rather, baptism is the public confession of faith. It symbolizes a commitment by both God and the believer (see 1 Pet 3:21). The submission of the believer to the water of baptism represents his or her humble request to God for a conscience cleared of guilt because of Christ's atoning blood.[35] Baptism is an act of confession and utter dependence. In summary, baptism in the Bible is neither elevated to be the cause of conversion nor diminished to be a mere marker of inclusion in a nonsalvific covenant. Rather, baptism is a public profession of God's saving work in the life of the believer. It is the public initiation of the believer into the family of faith.

The Lord's Supper. Christians celebrate the Lord's Supper in obedience to Christ's command, "Do this in remembrance of me" (Luke 22:19; 1 Cor 11:24).[36] He said the bread was his body and the cup was the new covenant in his blood. While the command to take the bread and cup "in remembrance" of him does not appear in Matthew, Mark, or John, the Supper itself is clearly recorded in all four Gospels.[37] The night before he was betrayed and crucified, Jesus shared a meal with his disciples. The exact relationship of this meal to the Old Testament Passover meal has been long debated, but few would question the larger typological relationship between the Passover meal and the death foreshadowed by the last supper.[38] Jesus clearly referred to the celebration as a Passover feast in Matt 26:18–19. Paul referred to Christ as "our Passover Lamb" (1 Cor 5:7) and called the church to keep the Passover feast (metaphorically) by living together in lives of holiness, thereby expressing unity in love (see 1 Cor 10:17).

---

[35] Cf. Heb 10:22.
[36] For a concise yet full treatment of biblical, historical, theological, and practical issues surrounding the Lord's Supper, see Robert Letham, *The Lord's Supper* (Phillipsburg, NJ: P&R, 2001); and Thomas R. Schreiner and Matthew R. Crawford, *The Lord's Supper: Remembering and Proclaiming Christ Until He Comes* (Nashville: B&H, 2010). Some manuscripts omit the words in Luke's Gospel.
[37] Matt 26:17–30; Mark 14:12–26; Luke 22:7–38; John 13:1–17.
[38] See Exodus 12; cf. Exod 24:8. D. A. Carson (*Matthew*, in *Expositor's Bible Commentary*, vol. 8, ed. Frank E. Gaebelein [Grand Rapids: Zondervan, 1984], 528–32) concluded that the last supper was a Passover meal.

The Lord's Supper evidences the companionship Christians share in Christ and in his Spirit as well as in holiness and mutual love.

> The new rite Jesus institutes has links with redemption history. As the bread has just been broken, so will Jesus' body be broken; and just as the people of Israel associated their deliverance from Egypt with eating the paschal meal prescribed as a divine ordinance, so also Messiah's people are to associate Jesus' redemptive death with eating this bread by Jesus' authority.[39]

This witness is to continue until Christ returns.[40]

Proper Form. The Bible does not provide an exact form (protocol and words spoken while distributing the elements) for the celebration of the Lord's Supper. This reticence, combined with the widespread nature of the practice, suggests the Lord's Supper should probably remain simple in form. Elaborate rituals would require careful written instructions, like those associated with Old Testament feasts. But no such instructions are given in the New Testament.[41]

The elements presented by the New Testament for the Lord's Supper are bread and wine ("fruit of the vine," Matt 26:29). Although wine in the first century was fermented, the degree to which it was diluted is unknown. Certainly the Corinthians were able to get drunk from the wine reserved for the Lord's Supper, for which Paul rebuked them (see 1 Cor 11:21). Other aspects of the celebration included a prayer of thanks (Matt 26:27) and a hymn (Matt 26:30). Beyond this the accounts specify nothing about spoken words or means used while distributing the bread and wine.

Proper Participants. As with baptism the question of *who* should participate in the Lord's Supper (the subjects) is more important than the question of *how* to participate in

---

[39] Carson, *Matthew*, 536.
[40] 1 Cor 11:26.
[41] The first indications of the form of the Lord's Supper observances are found in late first- and early second-century sources—*The Didache, 1 Clement,* and *Ignatius' Letter to the Smyrneans.*

it (the mode or form). Paul taught the Corinthians that participating in the Supper testifies to participating in Christ's body and blood. It is the believer's subjective identification with Christ's saving work, represented objectively by the elements on the table. The one who takes the bread and the cup testifies to sharing in the fruits of Christ's death, including a communion with both God and fellow Christians through the Spirit. Clearly, then, "the church must require of all those who desire to celebrate the Lord's Supper a credible profession of faith."[42]

As Paul said poignantly, anyone who eats and drinks at the Lord's table without this faith "eats and drinks judgment on himself" (1 Cor 11:29). Because faith is required for those who celebrate the Lord's Supper, it must be reserved for those who have been baptized.

While no passage in the New Testament spells out a comparative time line for the believer's participation in both ordinances, baptism should probably occur near the time of conversion—and then only once—whereas the Lord's Supper should be repeated regularly as a continuing symbol of participating in Christ by faith. Those who look by faith to the body and blood of Christ for salvation are called to participate in this feast and to do so in remembrance of him and in expectation of that final day when, Jesus said, "I drink it anew with you in my Father's kingdom" (Matt 26:29). Jesus referred here to "the marriage supper of the Lamb" (Rev 19:9). Thus the Lord's Supper is a regular rehearsal of this great celebration in which all Christians will share the table with their heavenly host, the Lord Jesus Christ.

---

[42] Berkhof, *Systematic Theology*, 657.

4

The Membership of the Church

I n today's world the concept of membership makes one think of clubs and other voluntary associations. Such organizations existed in the world of the Bible too.[1] But the idea of membership is even more basic to mankind. Households and families have members. Races and tribes and clans have members. So do communities and parties and elite groups like orders, guilds, and councils. An even more basic meaning of *member* refers to the human person. Our bodies have members.[2] The Bible uses the concepts of "member" and "membership" in all these various ways.

The Bible also represents churches as composed of members. Combining the collective images of families, parties, and communities with the even more integrated image of an individual body and its various parts, the Bible presents the local church as an entity made up of multiple individuals yet so highly integrated they are identifiable as a unit. They are even said to be a part of one another.[3] When Jesus instructed his followers to seek out the brother who has sinned (Matt 18:15–21), he was presupposing such

---

[1] The synagogue of the Freedmen in Acts 6:9; the Pharisees and Sadducees; various courts, councils, and guilds. In the Old Testament there were members of brotherhoods of warriors (e.g., David's 30 men, 2 Sam 23:8–39) or prophets.
[2] Rom 6:12–19; 7:23; 12:4–5; 1 Cor 6:15; 12:12–27; Eph 4:16; Jas 3:6; 4:1.
[3] Rom 12:5.

an integrated conception of body membership. Actions of reproach and, ultimately, exclusion are to occur within the arena of a specific and identifiable group of people. In many other places in the New Testament, a church appears to be composed of a specific and identifiable group of people.[4]

From the earliest of times, local Christian churches were congregations of specific, identifiable people. Certain people would be known to make up (or belong to) a particular assembly, while everyone else would be known to be outside of (or not belong to) the assembly. So the censure Paul enjoined in 1 Corinthians 5, like Jesus in Matthew 18, envisions an individual being excluded not from a political community but from a particular kind of social community. None are extant, but physical lists of members may well have existed in the earliest Christian churches. Clearly, the keeping of lists was not unknown in churches. The early church kept lists of widows (1 Tim 5:9). God himself keeps a list of all who belong to the universal church in his book of life (Rev 20:12). Paul assumed that the Corinthians had identified a "majority" of a particular set of church members who were eligible to vote.

The idea of a clearly defined community of people is central to God's action in both the Old and New Testaments. As demonstrated with Noah and his family, Abraham and his descendants, the nation of Israel, and the New Testament church, God has chosen to maintain a distinct and separate people for the purpose of displaying his character. God has always intended for a sharp, bright line to distinguish those who trust in him from those who do not. The lives of Christians together display visibly the gospel they proclaim audibly.

Responsibilities and Duties of Membership

If the church, in fact, presents a glorious climax in God's plan, several questions arise: How does an individual know he or she belongs to the church? How can one become a part of it? What is entailed by membership?

---

[4] E.g., Acts 9:41; 12:1; 15:3,22; Eph 2:19; 3:6; 4:25; 5:30; Col 2:19; 3:15; 3 John 9.

The responsibilities and duties of members of a Christian church are simply the responsibilities and duties of Christians.[5] Church members, like Christians, are to be baptized and regularly to attend the Lord's Supper. They are to hear God's Word and to obey it. They are regularly to fellowship together for mutual edification. They are to love God, one another, and those outside their fellowship; and they are to evidence the fruit of the Spirit (Gal 5:22–23). They are to worship God in all the activities of their home, work, community, and life.[6]

Christians also have particular duties in relation to the congregation. "Christianity is a corporate matter, and the Christian life can be fully realized only in relationship to others."[7] The most fundamental duty Christians have in relation to the congregation is the duty regularly to attend gatherings of the congregation.[8] In general, membership duties can be divided into duties toward other members and duties toward pastors.

The duties and responsibilities church members have *toward one another* summarize the life of the new society that is the church. As followers of Jesus Christ, Christians are obliged to love one another.[9] Christians are members of one family, even of one another.[10] Absent a life of love for one another, what other duty of church members is satisfying or worthwhile? Love obligates the members of the church to

---

[5] For the teaching on the duties of church members by Benjamin Keach, Benjamin Griffith, the Charleston Association, Samuel Jones, W. B. Johnson, Joseph S. Baker, and Eleazer Savage, see Mark Dever, ed., *Polity: Biblical Arguments on How to Conduct Church Life* (Washington, DC: Center for Church Reform, 2001), 65–69, 103–5, 125–26, 148–51, 221–22, 276–79, 510–11.

[6] For more on church membership, see 9Marks Ejournal on Church Membership (May–June 2011); http://www.9marks.org/ejournal/church-membership-holding-body-together; accessed on July 20, 2011. Cf. Ben Merkle and John Hammett, eds., *Those Who Must Give an Account: A Study of Church Membership and Church Discipline* (Nashville: B&H, 2011).

[7] Erickson, *Theology*, 1058. For a careful study of this in Paul's epistles, see James Samra, *Being Conformed to Christ in Community: A Study of Maturity, Maturation and the Local Church in the Undisputed Pauline Epistles* (London; T&T Clark, 2006) especially pp. 133–70.

[8] Heb 10:25; cf. Ps 84:4,10; Acts 2:42.

[9] John 13:34–35; 15:12–17; Rom 12:9–10; 13:8–10; Gal 5:15; 6:10; Eph 1:15; 1 Pet 1:22; 2:17; 3:8; 4:8; 1 John 3:16; 4:7–12; cf. Ps 133.

[10] 1 Cor 12:13–27.

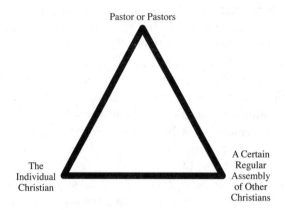

avoid anything that "tends to cool love."[11] By this love the nature of the gospel itself is demonstrated.

Church members are also obliged to seek peace and unity within their congregation.[12] The desire for peace and unity should follow naturally from the obligation to love.[13] Further, if Christians share the same spirit and mind—the Spirit of Christ—then unity is a natural expression of that Spirit. Given the sin which remains in believers in this life, however, unity often requires effort. Thus Christians "stand firm in one spirit, contending as one man for the faith of the gospel."[14] Strife should be actively avoided.[15]

Love is expressed and unity is cultivated when church members actively sympathize with one another. As Paul commanded the congregation in Rome, "Rejoice with those who rejoice; mourn with those who mourn."[16] Other duties follow: to care for one another physically and spiritually;[17] to

---

[11] Samuel Jones, *Treatise of Church Discipline* (1805) in *Polity: Biblical Arguments on How to Conduct Church Life,* ed. Mark Dever (Washington, DC: Center for Church Reform, 2001), 150; cf. 2 Cor 12:20; 1 Tim 5:13; 6:4; Jas 4:11.

[12] Rom 12:16; 14:19; 1 Cor 13:7; 2 Cor 12:20; Eph 4:3–6; Phil 2:3; 1 Thess 5:13; 2 Thess 3:11; Jas 3:18; 4:11.

[13] Rom 15:6; 1 Cor 1:10–11; Eph 4:5,13; Phil 2:2; cf. Zeph 3:9.

[14] Phil 1:27.

[15] Prov 17:14; Matt 5:9; 1 Cor 10:32; 11:16; 2 Cor 13:11; Phil 2:1–3.

[16] Rom 12:15; cf. Job 2:11; Isa 63:9; 1 Cor 12:26; Gal 6:2; 1 Thess 5:14; Heb 4:15; 12:3.

[17] Matt 25:40; John 12:8; Acts 15:36; Rom 12:13; 15:26; 1 Cor 16:1–2; Gal 2:10; 6:10; Heb 13:16; Jas 1:27; 1 John 3:17; cf. Deut 15:7–8,11.

watch over one another and hold one another accountable;[18] to work to edify one another;[19] to bear with one another,[20] including not suing one another;[21] to pray for one another;[22] to keep away from those who would destroy the church;[23] to reject evaluating people by worldly standards;[24] to contend together for the gospel;[25] and to be examples to one another.[26]

Church members also have particular responsibilities toward the leaders of the church, even as the leaders do to them. As Paul said to the Corinthians, "Men ought to regard us as servants of Christ and as those entrusted with the secret things of God."[27] Such men should be respected, held in the highest regard, and honored.[28] If Christians expect their pastor to fulfill his biblical responsibilities, church members must make themselves known to him. They must regard him as a gift from Christ sent to the church for their good.[29] The minister of the Word is a steward of God's household and an undershepherd of God's flock. He serves willingly and eagerly.[30] His reputation can and should be defended, his word believed, and his instructions obeyed unless Scripture is contradicted or facts are plainly distorted.[31] The faithful minister should be so regarded simply because he brings God's Word to his people; he does not replace it with his own.

Church members should remember their leaders and imitate their life and faith.[32] Good preachers and teachers are worthy of being doubly honored, according to Paul in

---

[18] Rom 15:14; Gal 6:1–2; Phil 2:3–4; 2 Thess 3:15; Heb 12:15; cf. Lev 19:17; Ps 141:5.
[19] 1 Cor 14:12–26; Eph 2:21–22; 4:12–29; 1 Thess 5:11; 1 Pet 4:10; 2 Pet 3:18.
[20] Matt 18:21–22; Mark 11:25; Rom 15:1; Gal 6:2; Col 3:12.
[21] 1 Cor 6:1–7.
[22] Eph 6:18; Jas 5:16.
[23] Rom 16:17; 1 Tim 6:3–5; Titus 3:10; 2 John 10–11.
[24] Matt 20:26–27; Rom 12:10–16; Jas 2:1–13.
[25] Phil 1:27; Jude 3.
[26] Phil 2:1–18.
[27] 1 Cor 4:1.
[28] Phil 2:29; 1 Thess 5:12–13.
[29] Similar to the way the apostles were to be regarded as delegates of Christ (Luke 10:16; cf. 1 Cor 16:10).
[30] 1 Pet 5:1–3.
[31] Heb 13:17,22; 1 Tim 5:17–19.
[32] 1 Cor 4:16; 11:1; Phil 3:17; Heb 13:7.

1 Tim 5:17, which includes material support.[33] And church members should give themselves both to praying for their ministers and to assisting them in every way they can.[34] Ministers of the Word have been given the task of bringing God's Word to God's people. As Paul said to the Corinthians, "We are therefore Christ's ambassadors, as though God were making his appeal through us. We implore you on Christ's behalf: Be reconciled to God."[35] More important work could hardly be conceived.

Responsibility and Duties of the Congregation as a Whole

In the New Testament local congregations realized they had particular responsibilities which could not be delegated to groups outside themselves. The local congregation was responsible for ensuring a qualified minister of the Word preached to them, insofar as it was in their power.[36] The congregation was ultimately responsible for ensuring converts were baptized and the Lord's Supper was duly administered to those giving credible evidence of regeneration. And the congregation was ultimately responsible for protecting and defining the membership of a church, both in admitting and dismissing members.[37] Thus Paul assigned these responsibilities to the Corinthian congregation in 1 Cor 5:1–13 and 2 Cor 2:1–11.

The entire congregation is also responsible for the faithful stewardship of the gifts entrusted to it. Foremost among these is the gospel, which must be preached in the church's own building, across the city, and around the world. Finally, the congregation is responsible for ensuring that the gospel message reaches out across these different spheres (see Gal 1:6–9; Phil 1:5; Col 1:3–4; 1 Thess 1:8).

---

[33] The word used in 1 Tim 5:17 for "honor" has a clear financial connotation; cf. Acts 6:4; 1 Cor 9:7–14; Gal 6:6.

[34] Eph 6:18–20; Col 4:3–4; 2 Thess 3:1; Heb 13:18–19.

[35] 2 Cor 5:20.

[36] We see this by inference from Gal 1:8 and 2 Tim 4:3, also Jude 3–4.

[37] Matt 18:17. Note the involvement of the whole church as the final court and as the executors of the discipline.

The congregation's responsibilities finally cannot be delegated. Though congregations may substitute the judgment of a body of leaders—whether inside or outside their number—the responsibility it bears is inescapable. Just as the people who paid the false teachers were threatened with God's judgment along with the teachers themselves (2 Tim 4:1–5), just as the Corinthian church was held accountable along with the sinning members (1 Cor 5:1–13), and just as the church envisioned in Matt 18:15–20 was held accountable by Christ to excluding the unrepentant, so congregations today cannot evade responsibility before God for fulfilling their biblically assigned duties.

What company is so obliged to worship God as those who have been not only created but redeemed? What group is so concerned with the task of proclamation of God's Word and evangelism as those who have themselves been saved through hearing the Word? What body will be so involved in making visible signs—in baptism and the Lord's Supper—of God's saving action in Christ? From the ministry of the Word to the management of the church's own affairs, what other group is so charged with responsibility as the church of Jesus Christ?[38]

---

[38] A good example of this is found in the details of Acts 15. Commenting on Acts 15:4, Jürgen Roloff wrote that "the full congregational assembly in Jerusalem comprises its own governing body, to be distinguished from the apostles and the elders as a governing body leading the Church. The apostolic decree concluded by them is determined by the entire congregational assembly" (J. Roloff, "ἐκκλησία," in *Exegetical Dictionary of the New Testament*, vol. 1, eds. Horst Balz and Gerhard Schneider [Grand Rapids: Eerdmans, 1990], 413–14).

5

The Polity of the Church

P olitics is the science of organizing life together. Normally it has to do with civil government, but interoffice, boardroom, and family politics are also commonly acknowledged. Once it is clear what a church is, the question naturally follows of how a church should be organized and led. These questions of the congregation's responsibilities and the role of the deacons and pastors are the subject of this chapter.

Congregationalism

The fundamental responsibility under God for the maintenance of all aspects of public worship of God belongs to the congregation. Whether in settling disputes between Christians (Matt 18:15–17; Acts 6:1–5), establishing correct doctrine (Gal 1:8; 2 Tim 4:3), or admitting and excluding members (2 Cor 2:6–8; 1 Cor 5:1–13), the local congregation has the duty and obligation to promote the continuance of a faithful gospel witness. No body outside of the whole congregation has this same degree of responsibility. While leaders within a congregation have their own special responsibilities before God, even the smallest of congregations which takes upon itself the task of providing and listening to the regular preaching of God's Word, and of practicing baptism and the Lord's Supper, necessarily takes upon itself responsibility for the right practice of membership and discipline, even over those who are called to be its leaders.[1]

While congregations may and do err in fulfilling these responsibilities, the responsibilities do not cease to belong to them. No other body, either inside or outside the local church, may finally remove these obligations of duty from the congregation as a whole. Toleration of erroneous teaching (particularly in regards to the gospel), neglect of baptism or the Lord's Supper, and carelessness in admitting or dismissing members are all the responsibility of the local congregation.[2]

Leadership in the Church

As with any gathered body of people, the church must be led. Universally and locally, the head and chief shepherd of the church is Christ.[3] Christ did not establish any sort of leadership structure, explicit or implicit, for the universal church during his earthly mission. Thus, between congregations of Christians, relationships are purely voluntary in nature.[4] Inside the local congregation, however, the New Testament's teaching is clear. The church is established with a simple order of leadership. Before turning to the specific offices established for the church in the New Testament, five biblical principles of such leadership should be considered for those who serve in leadership.

Church leaders should be *explicitly qualified*. Not all Christians are qualified to serve as leaders or overseers in the church. In Acts 20:17–38; 1 Tim 3:1–13; Titus 1:5–9; and 1 Pet 5:1–4, characteristics are laid down for undershepherds or elders of the flock. Distinctive among these qualifications is the requirement that those who serve as

---

[1] 1 Tim 5:19–20. For more on congregationalism, see Mark Dever, *A Display of God's Glory* 2nd ed. (Washington, DC: 9Marks Ministries, 2001), 31–43.

[2] Much of the New Testament's evidence from this comes in passages that address churches neglecting these duties.

[3] Eph 4:1–16; Heb 13:20; 1 Pet 5:4.

[4] This voluntary nature of relationships between congregations, however, does not mean that decisions made concerning one congregation's relations with another are simply indifferent matters.

overseers be "able to teach."[5] Furthermore, as representatives of Christ, elders or ministers have a special obligation to reflect the character of Christ. Such character will include a care for the flock, a willingness to serve, a lack of greed for money, a refusal to lord it over the flock, an exemplary life, blamelessness, being the husband of one wife,[6] and the ability to manage a household well. A minister is not overbearing, quick tempered, or given to much wine. And a minister should not be violent or willing to pursue dishonest gain. In these and other ways listed in Scripture, the leader in the congregation should be explicitly qualified.

Church leaders should be *reputable with outsiders*. Those who lead the church should not be men who bring the gospel into disrepute but men whose lives hold the gospel up as the glorious light of hope and truth in the world. God's heart of love for the world shines most clearly through pure lives. In order for the whole church to be oriented to its purpose, its leaders' interactions with the authorities, with neighbors, and with employers should commend the gospel to them. Paul said that overseers must not be lovers of money (1 Tim 3:3) but lovers of strangers (which is the meaning of the word "hospitable" in v. 2). In order faithfully to represent the Lord of the church, church leaders must have both God-centered and other-centered lives.

Church leaders should also possess *a keen sense of accountability*, knowing they are under authority themselves. Their lives as public leaders leave them open to public rebuke and correction.[7] The shepherds of the flock must realize they are stewards, not owners. Therefore they serve as undershepherds of God's flock, subject to his rule. This includes a realization of an ultimate accountability to Christ. James stated that teachers will be judged more strictly in the end,[8] while the author of Hebrews promised that church

---

[5] 1 Tim 3:2.
[6] Meaning not never divorced but rather faithful to his wife. There is no convincing reason to believe that Paul had in mind preconversion divorce or adultery any more than he would elsewhere have considered being disqualified due to other preconversion sins like lying, murder, or blasphemy.
[7] 1 Tim 5:19–20.
[8] Jas 3:1.

leaders will give an account to God for their work.[9] As John Brown said to one of his ministerial pupils who was newly ordained over a small congregation:

> I know the vanity of your heart, and that you will feel mortified that your congregation is very small, in comparison with those of your brethren around you; but assure yourself on the word of an old man, that when you come to give an account of them to the Lord Christ, at his judgment-seat, you will think you have had enough.[10]

This eschatological reality should have present implications in a minister's life and work. Those who lead others well must themselves first follow well. They must be submitted to Christ so that they can say, like Paul to the Corinthians, "Follow my example, as I follow the example of Christ" (1 Cor 11:1). Peter also reminded the church's undershepherds of their future appearance before Christ, bringing to mind the reward and the accounting they will give one day for their present work.[11]

Church leaders should exercise *authority*. While this observation may seem obvious, some dislike using words like "leader" or "authority" in the context of a local church. Perhaps they assume it implies a Diotrophes-like love to be first, or they associate it with un-Christlike boasting.[12] Yet Paul explicitly told Timothy, "If anyone sets his heart on being an overseer, he desires a noble task."[13] He told the Romans that those who are set over others (*proistamenos*) should use their gifts and abilities for the church.[14] He also exhorted Timothy to honor those "who direct the affairs of the church."[15] The writer to the Hebrews spoke about

---

[9] Heb 13:17.
[10] Cited by Alexander Grossart in *Works of Richard Sibbes,* ed. Alexander Grossart (1862–1864; repr. Edinburgh: Banner of Truth Trust, 1979), 294.
[11] 1 Pet 5:4.
[12] 3 John 9; 1 Cor 1–3.
[13] 1 Tim 3:1.
[14] Rom 12:8.
[15] 1 Tim 5:17.

"leaders."[16] All these words imply both the responsibility and initiative that should mark the actions of church leaders.

Finally, church leaders should *edify* the church. Genuine leadership not only requires a man to act with initiative and responsibility in an attempt to effect good, it also requires the accomplishment of that good. The ability to achieve the intended ends corroborates an individual's gifts and calling to leadership in the church. Leadership does not fundamentally depend on a self-proclaimed leader's own sense of internal calling and purpose. In 1 Corinthians 14, Paul repeatedly submits the putative gifts of the Spirit to the simple test of edification. He asks whether good fruit has been born in the church. Is the fruit of this person's action a church being built up? If this is the fruit of their actions, then they should be regarded highly, for the sake of the church and ultimately for the sake of Christ. All these characteristics should be present in those who lead a congregation.

Officers

Scripture provides for two specific offices in the local congregation: deacons and elders.[17]

Deacons

In modern translations of the New Testament, the word *diakonos* is usually translated "servant," sometimes "minister," and occasionally "deacon." The word can refer to service in general,[18] to rulers in particular,[19] and to caring for physical needs.[20] Women clearly serve this way in the New Testament.[21] Angels also serve in this way.[22] Sometimes the

---

[16] ἡγουμένοις; Heb 13:17,24.
[17] See Mark Dever, *A Display of God's Glory* (Washington, DC: 9Marks Ministries, 2001), 5–30. For a longer, careful treatment of these two offices, see Benjamin L. Merkle, *40 Questions About Elders and Deacons* (Grand Rapids: Kregel, 2008).
[18] Acts 1:17,25; 19:22; Rom 12:7; 1 Cor 12:5; 16:15; Eph 4:12; Col 4:17; 2 Tim 1:18; Phlm 13; Heb 6:10; 1 Pet 4:10–11; Rev 2:19.
[19] Rom 13:4.
[20] Matt 25:44; Acts 11:29; 12:25; Rom 15:25,31; 2 Cor 8:4,19–20; 9:1,12–13; 11:8.
[21] Matt 8:15 [Mark 1:31; Luke 4:39]; Matt 27:55 [Mark 15:41; cf. Luke 8:3]; Luke 10:40; John 12:2; Rom 16:1.
[22] Matt 4:11 [Mark 1:13].

word refers specifically to waiting on tables,[23] and though such service was despised in the Roman world, Jesus regarded it differently. In John 12:26 Jesus said, "Whoever *deacons* me must follow me; and where I am, my *deacon* also will be. My Father will honor the one who *deacons* me." Again in Matt 20:26 Jesus said, "Whoever wants to become great among you, must be your *deacon*." And in Matt 23:11 he said that "the greatest among you will be your *deacon*."

Jesus presents himself as a type of deacon.[24] Christians are presented as deacons of Christ or his gospel. The apostles are similarly depicted (Acts 6:1–7), and it is how Paul regularly referred to himself and to those who work with him.[25] He especially referred to himself as a deacon among the Gentiles, the particular group he was called to serve.[26] Paul called Timothy a deacon of Christ,[27] and Peter said that the Old Testament prophets were deacons to Christians.[28] Angels are called deacons.[29] Even Satan has his deacons.[30]

The clearest picture of the diaconal office in practice is found in Acts 6, where the first deacons were set aside. Based on that account, three aspects of a deacon's ministry may be noted.[31] First, deacons must care for physical needs. Some of the Christians "were being overlooked in the daily distribution of food" (v. 1). In v. 2, the apostles characterized this service as "waiting on tables," or literally, "deaconing tables." Caring for people, especially for other members of the congregation, contributes not only to their physical well-being but also to their spiritual well-being. It encourages the recipients of this care, it embodies God's care, and it acts as a witness to those outside the church. As Jesus said, "This is how the world will know that you are my disciples, by the love you

---

[23] Matt 22:13; Luke 10:40; 17:8; John 2:5,9; 12:2.
[24] Matt 20:28 [Mark 10:45; Luke 22:26–27; cf. John 13]; Luke 12:37; Rom 15:8.
[25] Acts 20:24; 1 Cor 3:5; 2 Cor 3:3,6–9; 4:1; 5:18; 6:3–4; 11:23; Eph 3:7; Col 1:23; 1 Tim 1:12; 2 Tim 4:11.
[26] Acts 21:19; Rom 11:13.
[27] 1 Tim 4:6; 2 Tim 4:5.
[28] 1 Pet 1:12.
[29] Heb 1:14.
[30] 2 Cor 11:15; Gal 2:17.
[31] Thanks to Buddy Gray, a pastor in Birmingham, Alabama, for pointing this out to me in the text.

have for one another."[32] The physical care presented in Acts 6 demonstrates that kind of Christlike love.

Behind the physical care lies a second aspect of a deacon's work, one which benefits not just those in need but the whole body also: deacons must strive for the unity of the body. By caring for these widows, the deacons helped make the food distribution among the widows more equitable. This was important because the *physical* neglect was causing a *spiritual* disunity in the body (Acts 6:1). One group of Christians was complaining against another group, and this seems to be what arrested the attention of the apostles. The apostles were not merely interested in rectifying a problem in the church's benevolence ministry. They wanted to prevent a fracture in church unity and a particularly dangerous fracture between two ethnic groups. The deacons were appointed to head off disunity in the church. Their job was to act as the shock absorbers for the body.

At a third level the deacons were appointed to support the ministry of the apostles. In Acts 6:3, the apostles acknowledged that caring for physical needs is a responsibility of the church. In some sense, therefore, they themselves owned this responsibility. But in v. 3 they determined to turn this responsibility over to another group within the church. Thus, these deacons were not only helping the widows and the body as a whole; they were also helping support the leaders whose main obligations lay elsewhere. By their ministry to widows, the deacons supported the teachers of the Word in their ministry. In this sense deacons are fundamentally encouragers and supporters of the ministry of the elders.

This servant role was made a regular office in Christian congregations. By the time Paul wrote his first letter to Timothy, he could instruct Timothy on the qualifications for what had become the formal office of deacon. When Paul's list of qualifications in 1 Tim 3:8–13 is combined with the qualities of the individuals selected in Acts 6, it becomes apparent that deacons should be known as being full of the Holy Spirit. They minister to physical needs, but their

---

[32] John 13:35, author's translation.

ministry is a spiritual ministry. Deacons should be known as being full of wisdom. They should be chosen by the congregation with the congregation's full confidence. They should willingly and diligently take on responsibility for the needs of their particular ministry. They should be worthy of respect, sincere, not indulgent in much wine, not interested in dishonest gain, and steadfast in the deep truths of the faith with a clear conscience. Deacons should be tested and approved servants who are the husband of but one wife. And they should be individuals who manage their own children and household well.

In addition to the office of deacon, the New Testament provides for the office of pastor, elder, or bishop. Most fundamentally, the elder is a minister of the Word. The *presbeut*[33] root occurs 76 times in the New Testament. Nine occurrences refer to people of chronologically advanced age.[34] Four times it refers to ancestors of the Hebrew nation.[35] John used the word *presbuteros* 12 times in Revelation to refer to the heavenly elders.[36] This word also refers to the Jewish nonpriestly leaders in the Sanhedrin or in local synagogues 29 times (all in the Gospels and Acts). The remaining 20 uses refer to elders in churches: in the Jerusalem church;[37] in Lystra, Iconium, and Antioch;[38] in Ephesus;[39] in the towns of Crete;[40] and other general references.[41] John the apostle referred to himself twice as "the elder."[42] The Jews of Jesus' day had lay members of the Sanhedrin in Jerusalem called elders. Local synagogues also had bodies of ruling men called elders.

In the New Testament the words "elder," "shepherd" or "pastor," and "bishop" or "overseer" are used interchangeably in the context of the local church office.[43] This is seen

---

[33] πρεσβύτ.
[34] Luke 1:18; 15:25; John 8:9; Acts 2:17; 1 Tim 5:1,2; Titus 2:2,3; Phlm 9.
[35] Matt 15:2; Mark 7:3,5; Heb 11:2.
[36] Rev 4:4,10; 5:5,6,8,11,14; 7:11,13; 11:16; 14:3; 19:4.
[37] Acts 11:30; 15:2,4,6,22,23; 16:4; 21:18.
[38] Acts 14:21,23.
[39] Acts 20:17.
[40] Titus 1:5.
[41] 1 Tim 5:17,19; Jas 5:14; 1 Pet 5:1,5.
[42] 2 John 1; 3 John 1.
[43] See Benjamin L. Merkle, *The Elder and Overseer: One Office in the Early Church* (New York: Peter Lang, 2003).

most clearly in Acts 20, when Paul met with the "elders"[44] of the church in Ephesus (v. 17), as he called them. Paul said to these elders: "Keep watch over yourselves and all the flock of which the Holy Spirit has made you overseers [or bishops].[45] Be shepherds [or pastors][46] of the church of God, which he bought with his own blood" (v. 28). In Eph 4:11, Paul said that Christ "gave some to be apostles, some to be prophets, some to be evangelists, and some to be pastors and teachers." The word Paul used for "pastor" is *poimen*,[47] the word for "shepherd." Similarly, in 1 Pet 5:1–2, Peter addressed the elders, telling them to pastor or shepherd [again, this is the verb] God's flock, serving as overseers or bishops. In 1 Pet 2:25, Jesus is called the "Shepherd and Overseer of your souls." The root of the word translated "overseer" here (*episkop*)[48] occurs 11 times in the New Testament. In Titus 1:5–9, Paul provided a list of qualifications for a particular office similar to the one he gave in 1 Tim 3:1–7. In both places the officer described is called an *episkopos*, that is, a bishop or overseer. But in Titus 1:5, Paul also said that he left Titus in Crete in order to ensure *presbeuterous* ("elders") were in every town. Then in v. 7, he refers to the same person as an *episkopos*. Clearly, the New Testament refers interchangeably to elders, shepherds or pastors, and bishops or overseers in the context of the officers in the local church.[49]

Paul laid out the qualifications for elders in 1 Tim 3:1–7 and in Titus 1:5–9. Elders are to be blameless and above reproach, not overbearing, temperate, self-controlled, respectable, hospitable, able to teach, not given to much wine, not violent but gentle, not quarrelsome, well reputed (particularly among outsiders), upright, holy, and disciplined.

---

[44] πρεσβυτέροθς.

[45] ἐπισκόπους.

[46] ποιμαίνειν.

[47] ποιμήν.

[48] ἐπίσκοπ.

[49] So concluded R. B. C. Howell, pastor of First Baptist Church, Nashville, Tennessee: "The only officers appointed by God to preach, and administer ordinances, and whose commission has come down to our times, are called indifferently, elders, bishops and presbyters; all of which names, when referring to office, convey the same idea" (R. B. C. Howell, "Ministerial Ordination," in *The Baptist Preacher*, ed. Henry Keeling [Richmond: H. K. Ellyson, 1847], 137).

He is the husband of one wife, not a lover of money, not a pursuer of dishonest gain, a good manager of his family (his children obey him), and not a recent convert. He loves what is good, holds firmly to the gospel, and is eager to serve.[50]

All of the qualifications listed here are repeated elsewhere in Scripture as applicable for all Christians, except for not being a recent convert and being able to teach. The essence of the elder's office is found in teaching—ensuring the Word of God is well understood. Such a ministry of teaching would show itself in the commitment to that task among the members of one's own congregation. Anyone serving as an elder should have a better-than-average grasp of the basics of the gospel as well as the great truths of Scripture, especially those that are under assault in one's own day. An elder should also have a particularly solid grasp of those truths which distinguish his own congregation from others (e.g., baptism for Baptists). And he should be an example of care and concern for the congregation as a whole.

The qualification to be "the husband of but one wife" and to "manage his household well" does not mean that an elder must be married or have children.[51] Rather it appears Paul assumed that most men would be married and have children and that those family relations provide a natural ground for assessing a man's ability to lead. Paul also assumed that the elders would be men. Inherent in creation, Paul argued in 1 Tim 2:12–14, exists a divine order which precludes a woman from being called "to teach or to have authority over a man" in the church.[52]

Plurality of Elders. A common discussion about New Testament elders is whether each local congregation was governed by only one elder or multiple elders.

---

[50] For this last qualification, see 1 Pet 5:2.

[51] It would seem odd that any qualification for elder would rule out Paul himself from serving as an elder.

[52] Much helpful material on this has been published by the Council on Biblical Manhood and Womanhood. See John Piper and Wayne Grudem, eds., *Recovering Biblical Manhood and Womanhood* (Wheaton, IL: Crossway, 1991); and Wayne Grudem and Dennis Rainey, eds., *Pastoral Leadership for Manhood and Womanhood* (Wheaton, IL: Crossway, 2002).

Before Jesus established the church, the Jewish towns of Palestine were accustomed to being governed by multiple elders. Thus, in Luke 7:3, the centurion sent several elders of the local Jewish community in Capernaum to Jesus to plead on his behalf for help. Deuteronomy also refers to multiple elders in the context of their role as town leaders, whether that involves retrieving people from cities of refuge, solving murders, or dealing with disobedient children (19:12; 21:1–9,18–21). Jewish synagogues similarly followed a pattern of plural leadership. Arising during the Babylonian exile, synagogues functioned as the religious and civil gathering for teaching God's law and, consequently, leading the community. Ten adult males were required to establish a synagogue for public worship. Various offices facilitated the work of synagogues, including the office of ruler.[53]

The evidence suggests that New Testament congregations also were generally led by more than one elder. Five New Testament authors refer to the office a total of 20 times.

James, Peter, Paul, and Luke also referred to the office of elder in the church, and each of them apparently presumed a plurality of elders per congregation.[54] James instructed his Christian reader to "call the elders [plural] of the church [singular] to pray over him" (Jas 5:14). Peter wrote as an elder to the "elders [plural] among you" (1 Pet 5:1–5). Unless Peter was saying, "from one old man to others," then he assumed a plurality of elders existed within each congregation. Paul greeted "the overseers" (plural) in the church (singular) at Philippi (Phil 1:1). And he exhorted the elders of the church at Ephesus to be "overseers" (plural) for the "flock" (singular) to which God had called them (Acts 20:28). Writing to Timothy and Titus, Paul again mentioned elders in the plural. He reminded Timothy of the body of elders who laid their hands on him (1 Tim 4:14). A little later

---

[53] Examples of the "rulers" of synagogues mentioned in the New Testament are Jairus in Mark 5:22 (plural rulers); Acts 13:15 (plural); Crispus in Acts 18:8 (singular).

[54] John alone referred to the office exclusively in the singular. He referred to himself as "the elder" in his second and third letters (2 John 1; 3 John 1). Apparently, he was known by this title. Assuming he wrote to people outside of his own congregation, the title may have suggested not so much an office as his wide recognition.

he referred to the elders (plural) who direct the affairs of the church (singular) (5:17). And then he referred to accusations—not against "the elder"—but against "an elder" (5:19; *presbeuterou*, without an article), which would be consistent with the assumption that Timothy had multiple elders in his one congregation.

Paul also left Titus in Crete in order to "appoint elders [plural] in every town" [*kata polin*, read distributively, "in *each* town"] (Titus 1:5), again probably meaning that Paul intended each church in Crete to have a plurality of elders. Finally, Luke's narrative in Acts gives evidence for a plurality of elders in each local congregation. The church (singular) in Ephesus had multiple elders (Acts 20:17). At the end of Paul's first missionary journey, "Paul and Barnabas appointed elders [plural] for them in each church [singular]" (Acts 14:23). And references to the elders of the Jerusalem church always occur in the plural.[55] Therefore, the direct evidence in the New Testament indicates that the common and even expected practice was to have a plurality of elders in each local congregation.[56]

Senior Pastor? Another question that naturally arises these days is whether the New Testament supports the position of a senior or sole pastor. While no direct New Testament evidence points to this distinction, four glimpses can be found for a leading teacher among the elders, even in these early congregations. First, some men in the New Testament, like Timothy or Titus, moved from place to place yet served as elders. Other men would have remained in one location, perhaps like the men appointed by Titus in every town (Titus 1:5). In other words, Timothy set a precedent by coming from outside the community to act in a leadership role, even while other leaders were already in place. Apparently, outsiders are not excluded from joining a community in order to assume primary teaching responsibilities.

---

[55] Acts 11:30; 15:2,4,6,22–23; 16:4; 21:18.
[56] The Anglican scholar and pioneer missiologist Roland Allen came to this same conclusion: "St. Paul was not content with ordaining one Elder for each Church. In every place he ordained several. This ensured that all authority should not be concentrated in the hands of one man" (Roland Allen, *Missionary Methods: St. Paul's or Ours?* [London: Robert Scott, 1912], 138–39).

Second, some men were financially supported for full-time work with the flock,[57] while other men simultaneously remained in their vocations and performed their work as elders. Paul often did this when establishing the gospel in a new area. Could every elder in the new Christian congregations in the villages of Crete have been fully supported?

Third, Paul wrote to Timothy alone with instructions for the Ephesian church, even though the book of Acts clearly points to a plurality of elders in the Ephesian church. Apparently, Timothy played a unique role among them.

Finally, Jesus addressed his letters to the seven churches in Revelation 2–3 to the "angel" or "messenger" (singular) of each of these churches.

None of these examples present an explicit command, but they describe the common practice of setting aside at least one individual from among the elders potentially from outside the congregation's community, supporting that individual, and giving him the primary teaching responsibility in the church. Nevertheless, the preacher, or pastor, is fundamentally one of the elders of his congregation. Working together with that senior pastor, the plurality of elders aid both him and the church by rounding out the pastor's gifts, making up for his shortcomings, supplementing his judgment, and creating support in the congregation for decisions, leaving leaders less exposed to unjust criticism. A plurality also makes leadership more rooted and permanent, and it allows for more mature continuity. It encourages the church to take more responsibility for the spiritual growth of its own members and helps make the church less dependent on its employees. As the elders lead and the deacons serve, the congregation is prepared to live as the witness God intends his church to be.

Elder Ruled or Elder Led? Two churches which both have a plurality of elders may still be very different. Who may serve as elders? How are they recognized? How long

---

[57] E.g., Phil 4:15–18; 1 Tim 5:17–18. The "especially" in 1 Tim 5:17 would be better translated as "I mean." Paul was restating and clarifying here, as he did when he used the same word in 4:10. Paul did not advocate a separate class of elders who did not teach but who only ruled.

do they serve? Must they be recognized by any group outside the local church? What is their authority individually,
and what authority only resides in the eldership as a whole?
Are decisions made by consensus, unanimity, or a majority?
Perhaps most importantly, what is their role and authority
relative to the congregation's authority?

Some Christians argue that the elder is called to rule or
direct the affairs of the local church, based on passages like
1 Tim 5:17; Titus 1:7; and Heb 13:7,17. The congregation's
responsibility, they would say, is only and always to submit to
them.[58] This position is called *elder rule*. Advocates of elder
rule don't claim, of course, that the eldership will always be
correct; they simply say that it will be God's responsibility
finally to assess and judge them. The elders are clearly called
to teach and lead; the congregation to submit and follow.

Still other Christians consider those same passages
about the leadership responsibilities of the elders and say
that Scripture also gives certain responsibilities to the congregation as a whole. They point to the same passages that
have been mentioned earlier, passages affirming the congregation's oversight in matters of membership (2 Cor 2:6–7),
discipline (Matt 18:15–20; 1 Corinthians 5), and the right
preaching of the gospel (Gal 1:7–8; 2 Tim 4:3). The final
responsibility of the congregation does not contradict or
undermine the elders' general leadership, but it provides an
opportunity to confirm it when it is right and to constrain it
when it is in error. This position is called *elder led*.

Rather than seeing a senior pastor as being in competition with a group of elders, or the elders and the congregation
disputing about limits of authority and responsibility, this
last position, which is my own, posits that they can all work
well together. The congregation recognizes and submits
to the elders. On matters that are important and clear, the
elders and congregation should normally agree; and when
they do not, the authority of the congregation is final. On
matters that are less clear, the congregation should trust the
elders and go along with them, trusting God's providential

---

[58] A recently published example of this position is Ted Bigelow, *The Titus Mandate*
(self-published, 2011).

work through them. Churches always benefit from clearly delineating and agreeing upon everyone's responsibilities and obligations.

While members of a church must agree on their own structures of authority, churches with different polities may still partner together in a number of areas. Polity disagreements may preclude planting churches together, but it does not preclude partnering for pastoral fellowship, education, evangelistic work, Bible translation, or various social ministries. Certainly it is never appropriate for churches to remove their affections from one another over differences in polity. In a healthy local church, a biblical polity will bring peace to the congregation as well as to that congregation's fellowship with other evangelical churches.

6

The Discipline of the Church

Old Testament

In the Old Testament, God called Abraham and his descendants to be his special people. However, God's holy presence with this people required a special holiness on their part.[1] "The LORD said to Moses, 'Speak to the entire assembly of the house of Israel and say to them: "Be holy because I, the LORD your God, am holy."'"[2] Their holiness should reflect his own. God continued to preserve this witness for himself to the nations through the establishment of the covenant at Mount Sinai—detailed in Exodus, Leviticus, Numbers, and Deuteronomy—and into the time of the writing prophets.

During the centuries between Moses and Ezra, Israel existed as a testimony of God's faithfulness to his promises to Abraham. Individuals are excluded from the community by means of the Levitical code if their lives became too polluted. Gordon Wenham summarized the purpose of the Levitical code: "The unclean and the holy are two states which must never come in contact with each other."[3] An individual is temporarily excluded from God's people for a

---

[1] Exod 33:14–16.
[2] Lev 19:1–2; see 11:44–45; 20:26.
[3] Gordon J. Wenham, *The Book of Leviticus*, New International Commentary on the Old Testament (Grand Rapids: Eerdmans, 1979), 19–20.

number of different actions.[4] For other more serious sins, capital punishment was required,[5] as was a divine severing from the Abrahamic promises (e.g., being "cut off" from God's people).[6] It is an honor to belong to God's people, and membership has both obligations and privileges.

Ultimately, the nation's sins became too great for God to tolerate, so he judged the whole nation. First, the nation was divided. Then, after more centuries of disobedience, the northern tribes fell to Assyria, and later the southern tribes fell to Babylon. If his people would not live distinctly from the nations—if instead they adopt the immorality and idolatry of those nations—then his people would be dispersed among them. God would not allow them to continue forever bearing his name in vain. In Ezekiel, God summarized the history of his faithfulness despite the people's unfaithfulness: "The people of Israel rebelled against me in the desert. They did not follow my decrees but rejected my laws—although the man who obeys them will live by them. . . . So I said I would pour out my wrath on them and destroy them in the desert. But for the sake of my name I did what would keep it from being profaned in the eyes of the nations in whose sight I had brought them out."[7]

New Testament

In the New Testament, the church is also to exercise discipline because an expectation of holiness remains on God's people. "As obedient children, do not conform to the evil desires you had when you lived in ignorance. But just as he who called you is holy, so be holy in all you do; for it is written, 'Be holy, because I am holy.'"[8] The church was founded by Christ, and its success is promised and ensured by him.[9] He commits to form holiness in his people through his Spirit.

---

[4] See Leviticus 11–15, 18.
[5] Lev 17:10; 20:3–5.
[6] E.g., Exod 30:38; Lev 7:20–21; Num 15:30–31.
[7] Ezek 20:13–14.
[8] 1 Pet 1:14–16 (quoting Lev 11:44–45; 19:2; 20:7).
[9] Matt 16:17–19.

Christ's Spirit uses the local body of believers to form and maintain the special holiness of God's people, in part through the exercise of church discipline. The writer to the Hebrews reminded young Christians about the importance of discipline in the Christian life.[10] Part of that discipline occurs through the interaction of the people, as one member of Christ's body cares for another. So Paul wrote to the Galatians, "Brothers, if someone is caught in a sin, you who are spiritual should restore him gently. But watch yourself, or you also may be tempted. Carry each other's burdens, and in this way you will fulfill the law of Christ."[11] He also warned the Thessalonians to

> keep away from every brother who is idle and does not live according to the teaching you received from us. . . . If anyone does not obey our instruction in this letter, take special note of him. Do not associate with him, in order that he may feel ashamed. Yet do not regard him as an enemy, but warn him as a brother.[12]

And to Titus, Paul instructed, "Warn a divisive person once, and then warn him a second time. After that, have nothing to do with him.[13]

Matthew 18

This concept of church discipline, which can culminate in exclusion from the church, originated in the teaching of Christ himself. In Matthew 18, Jesus taught on the nature of following him, instructing about love which seeks the lost and mercy toward others. In the same context he also explained what should be done when one of his followers sins against another.

> If your brother sins against you, go and show him his fault, just between the two of you. If he listens to you, you have won your brother over. But if he will not

---

[10] Heb 12:1–14.
[11] Gal 6:1–2.
[12] 2 Thess 3:6,14–15; cf. 1 Tim 1:20; 5:19–20.
[13] Titus 3:10.

> listen, take one or two others along, so that "every
> matter may be established by the testimony of two
> or three witnesses." If he refuses to listen to them,
> tell it to the church; and if he refuses to listen even
> to the church, treat him as you would a pagan or a
> tax collector.[14]

Christ gave three steps for confronting someone who both
claims to be his follower and yet refuses to repent of sin—
first private confrontation, then small group confrontation,
and finally congregational confrontation. While these steps
may be more suggestive than exhaustive, the desired out-
come at each stage of confrontation is the same: the disciple's repentance.[15] However, should the one sinning even
refuse to listen to the church, then he should be treated as "a
pagan or a tax collector." He has demonstrated that he does
not belong in the church because he is not characterized by
holy repentance.

Discipline is inextricably bound up with the church
Jesus envisioned. But that discipline should not occur alone.
Rather, it should occur as one part of a larger commitment
by the entire church to pray and work for one another's for-
mation in Christ. A rejection of such fashioning must be met
by the lamentable rejection from the community which is
defined by it.

1 Corinthians 5

Perhaps the most cited text on the practice of excommunication or church discipline is 1 Corinthians 5. In this
passage Paul specifically directs the entire congregation to
"expel the wicked man from among you" (v. 13). Paul took
these words from Deuteronomy, where the Lord instructed
his people through Moses to expel those who worshipped
other gods, who gave a false witness, and who practiced
premarital sex, adultery, or certain kinds of slavery.[16] In
ancient Israel such exclusion might have been carried out

---

[14] Matt 18:15–17.
[15] E.g., "Hand this man over to Satan, so that the sinful nature may be destroyed
and his spirit saved on the day of the Lord" (1 Cor 5:5).
[16] Deut 17:7; 19:19; 22:21,24; 24:7.

through capital punishment. Paul, in his exhortation to the Corinthian congregation, simply meant that the offender should be expelled from his community, similar to Jesus' command in Matt 18:17 for the unrepentant sinner to be treated as a pagan or a tax collector. Though the offender claimed to be a Christian, his claim held no credence given his evident lack of repentance. Such judging inside the church is actually a part of the work of the church, said Paul: "What business is it of mine to judge those outside the church? Are you not to judge those inside?"[17] "Yes" is the answer Paul assumed to this second rhetorical question.

The nature of the exclusion Paul enjoined is excommunication, which typically means excluding the parties in question from communion (the Lord's Supper). In essence, this is a removal from church membership. While other disciplinary situations might call for a gradual approach, with something like a warning followed by a temporary suspension from certain privileges of membership, Paul contemplated no such middle steps in 1 Corinthians 5. The crime was heinous and public, and the church's response needed to be equally public and decisive.[18] Hence, Paul took excommunication in this circumstance beyond a mere denial of the Lord's Supper to the unrepentant. He wrote, "I am writing you that you must not associate with anyone who calls himself a brother but is sexually immoral or greedy, an idolater or a slanderer, a drunkard or a swindler. With such a man do not even eat."[19] He reacted strongly because the sinner's unrepentant life contrasted so starkly with his claim to be a Christian. As long as the church allowed him to remain in membership, it affirmed this claim and

---

[17] 1 Cor 5:12.

[18] Traditionally Christians have made a distinction between public and private offenses. Public offenses were addressed with Paul's counsel in 1 Corinthians 5, in which no private rebukes preceded the public one. Private offenses were addressed with Jesus' words in Matthew 18, in which a series of private appeals are made before being brought to public attention. For more on this distinction, see P. H. Mell and Eleazer Savage (among others) in their teaching reprinted in *Polity: Biblical Arguments on How to Conduct Church Life*, ed. Mark Dever (Washington, DC: Center for Church Reform, 2001), 422–26, 485–86, 520. Cf. Jonathan Leeman, *Church Discipline: How the Church Protects the Name of Jesus* (Wheaton, IL: Crossway, 2012), chap. 3.

[19] 1 Cor 5:11.

simultaneously provided the world with a deeply distorted picture of what a Christian is. The original sin belonged to the sinning couple. But the sin which drew Paul's ire and sharp tone was the inaction of the congregation. Their failure to act was potentially disastrous to their gospel witness and amounted to neglect of the gospel, which in itself is a serious sin. Church discipline done correctly might bring a sinner to repentance, but it will always faithfully represent the gospel to the surrounding community.[20]

Finally, church discipline should be practiced in order to bring sinners to repentance, a warning to other church members, health to the whole congregation, a distinct corporate witness to the world, and, ultimately, glory to God, as his people display his character of holy love.[21]

---

[20] "Beware of an ambition for mere numbers: a small body of well-instructed, earnest disciples is worth far more to the cause of Christ than a heterogeneous multitude undistinguished in spirit and life from the world" (H. Harvey, *The Pastor: His Duties and Qualifications* [Philadelphia: American Baptist Publication Society, 1879], 66).

[21] See Matt 5:16; 1 Pet 2:12.

7

The Purpose of the Church

The topics already covered within this book cannot be fully appreciated apart from a concrete understanding of the purpose of the church. The church's purpose lies at the heart of its nature, attributes, and marks and right practices of membership, polity, and discipline serve those purposes. The proper ends for a local congregation's life and actions are the worship of God, the edification of the church, and the evangelization of the world.[1] These three purposes in turn serve the glory of God.

Preaching and Worship

The collective worship of God occurs in the context of the assembled congregation while individual worship of God occurs in the context of one's daily life. Shaping and encouraging both corporate and individual worship are significant aspects of the church's purpose.

Assembled Worship: Elements

The worship of God in the public assembly consists of the particular elements prescribed by God within a particular

---

[1] Among important passages that stand as a background to what God is doing with his people are the following: Exod 19:5–6; Mark 13:10; 14:9; Matt 28:16–20; Luke 4:16–21; 24:44–49; John 20:21; Acts 1:8; Eph 3:10–11.

set of historical circumstances. God's Word should direct a church's corporate worship. As David Peterson wrote, "The worship of the living and true God is essentially an engagement with him on the terms that he proposes and in the way that he alone makes possible."[2] Ligon Duncan summarized what elements should be included in corporate worship with the motto, "Read the Bible, preach the Bible, pray that Bible, sing the Bible and see the Bible."[3] By "seeing" the Bible, Duncan referred to the celebration of baptism and the Lord's Supper, which depict the gospel. Since this aspect of corporate worship is considered above, the remaining elements of corporate worship to be considered here are reading the Bible, preaching the Bible, singing the Bible, and praying the Bible.

Christians are commanded to read the Bible when assembled for worship. Paul exhorted Timothy, "Devote yourself to the public reading of Scripture."[4]

But God's Word must not only be read; it must also be explained and applied. Hence, right preaching of God's Word is central to the church's worship, forming its basis and core. Since faith comes by hearing God's Word (Rom 10:14–17), Scripture must be explained with precision and passion. So Paul exhorted Timothy, "Preach the Word; be prepared in season and out of season; correct, rebuke and encourage— with great patience and careful instruction."[5]

The duty of singing God's praises is enjoined upon Christians by both example and command. Matthew and Mark record, for instance, the fact that Jesus and the

---

[2] David Peterson, *Engaging with God* (Downers Grove: IVP, 1992), 20. Cf. D. A. Carson's much longer definition, in D. A. Carson, ed., *Worship by the Book* (Grand Rapids: Zondervan, 2002), 30.

[3] J. Ligon Duncan, "Foundations for Biblically Directed Worship," in *Give Praise to God: A Vision for Reforming Worship*, ed. P. G. Ryken, D. W. H. Thomas, and J. L. Duncan III (Phillipsburg: P&R, 2003), 65. A strong case can also be made for regarding financial giving as an element of public worship because of Paul's instructions to the Corinthian church (1 Cor 16:1–2; 2 Cor 9:6–7). The early Christians gave benevolently toward those in need (e.g., Matt 5:42; 6:3; Luke 6:38; 21:1–4; Acts 4:34–35; 11:29; 20:35; Rom 12:8). What is unclear is the association of this act of Christian worship with the public gathering of the assembly.

[4] 1 Tim 4:13; see Ezra's ministry of reading the law publicly (Nehemiah 8).

[5] 2 Tim 4:2.

disciples sang a hymn after the last supper.[6] Paul instructed
the Ephesian congregation, "Speak to one another with
psalms, hymns and spiritual songs. Sing and make music
in your heart to the Lord, always giving thanks to God
the Father for everything, in the name of our Lord Jesus
Christ."[7] Ultimately, the praises of the Christian assembly on
earth foreshadow the praise which will be offered in heaven.[8]

Another element of gathered Christian worship is
prayer. In prayer Christians glorify God in a number of ways:
by making known their reliance on him, by demonstrating
obedience to his command to pray, by remembering his
faithfulness to answer previous prayers, and by relying on
his kindness in asking for still more.

In corporate prayer God is magnified while the church
is edified and encouraged. Jesus taught his followers to
pray in a corporate fashion beginning with "Our Father."[9]
James urged early Christians to "confess your sins to each
other and pray for each other so that you may be healed."[10]
The book of Acts is also full of prayer. The early Christians
"devoted themselves to the apostles' teaching and to the fellowship, to the breaking of bread and to prayer."[11] Reading
and preaching God's Word, singing his praises, and praying
to him are the required elements in the weekly gathering of
Christians.

Behind the assertion that Christian worship must consist of these God-prescribed elements is the Protestant
understanding of the sufficiency of Scripture—the idea that
the Scriptures sufficiently reveal everything God's people
need for salvation, perfect trust, and perfect obedience. The
sufficiency of Scripture has many implications, including
the conviction that Scripture should regulate the way God's
people should approach God in worship. This principle has
often been called "the regulative principle." The regulative
principle applies the Protestant belief in the authority of

[6] Matt 26:30; Mark 14:26.
[7] Eph 5:19–20; cf. Col 3:16.
[8] Rev 5:9–14.
[9] Matt 6:7–15; Luke 11:1–4.
[10] Jas 5:16; cf. Eph 6:18; Phil 4:6; Col 4:2; 1 Thess 5:17; 1 Tim 2:8; Jas 5:13.
[11] Acts 2:42; cf. 1:14; 4:24–31; 12:5,12.

God's Word to the particular doctrine of the church (most often it is referenced in discussions of public worship).

Many people have debated what specific applications should be drawn from the regulative principle for the weekly gathering of the saints. For example, does the principle require or forbid taking an offering during a service? having a choir? using drama in lieu of a sermon? and so forth. Yet before the particular points of application are tackled, the basic principle should be clearly and firmly set in place: God has revealed what basic components of worship are acceptable to him. Left to themselves humans do not worship God as they should, not even those who are blessed by him. One needs only to think of the unacceptable sacrifice of Cain or the golden calf of the Israelites.

In response to humanity's lack of knowledge and desire to worship him rightly, God graciously grants humanity his Word. The first two of the Ten Commandments show God's concern for how he is to be worshipped.[12] Jesus condemned the Pharisees for aspects of their worship.[13] Paul instructed the church at Corinth on what should and should not occur in their assemblies.[14] In short, recognizing the regulative principle amounts to recognizing the sufficiency of Scripture applied to assembled worship.[15] In the language of the Reformation, it amounts to *sola scriptura*.

Assembled Worship: Circumstances

The time and place for assembled Christian worship are not clearly prescribed in the New Testament. Both public places (like the temple or a riverside) and private spaces (like homes) are used.[16] Nor does the New Testament have anything to say on numerous other matters of circumstance,

---

[12] Exod 20:2–4; Deut 5:6–10. These commands were violated many times throughout the Old Testament, e.g. Lev 10:1–3; Deut 4:2; 12:32; 1 Sam 15:22; 2 Samuel 6; Jer 19:5; 32:35. All of these stories (Nadab and Abihu, Saul, and Uzzah) show that right intention by itself is insufficient for right worship.
[13] Matt 15:1–14.
[14] First Corinthians 11–14.
[15] For more on the regulative principle, see the first two chapters in Ryken, Thomas, and Duncan, *Give Praise to God*, and D. A. Carson's introduction to his *Worship by the Book*.
[16] E.g., Acts 2:46; 4:31; 5:42; 16:13; Rom 16:5.

such as whether microphones can be used to amplify voices or the order in which those elements should occur when the church gathers. Answering circumstantial questions like these must inevitably depend on a church's prudence.

Having said that, the church throughout its history has deemed it appropriate to meet on Sunday for several reasons. First, Christ was raised on a Sunday.[17] Second, the risen Christ first met the disciples on a Sunday.[18] Third, the pattern of the first Christians in the New Testament points toward Sunday as the weekly time for a worship gathering, even though Sunday would not have been a day of rest for them.[19] Fourth, this pattern was quickly enshrined in language with references to Sunday as "the Lord's day."[20] According to early sources in the Christian church, this was the universal custom of Christians.[21] Finally, Christians throughout history have deemed it appropriate to give the firstfruits of the week to God in order to acknowledge his ownership of the whole, just as they do with income.

Individual Worship

In addition to promoting and regulating the corporate worship of God by the assembly, the church's mission purpose includes fostering the individual's worship of God. Worship does not only occur in public services and assemblies. It should occur in the Christian's daily living. So Paul exhorted the Christians in Rome, "Offer your bodies as living sacrifices, holy and pleasing to God—this is your spiritual act of worship."[22] Theology lived out in responsible action and obedience is worshipping God. When performed in faith, all the duties of the Christian life commanded in Scripture are means of worshipping God. "And whatever

---

[17] Matt 28:1–2; Mark 16:2–5; Luke 24:1–3; John 20:1.
[18] Matt 28:8–10; John 20:13–19; cf. Luke 24:13–15.
[19] Acts 20:7; 1 Cor 16:1–2.
[20] Rev 1:10.
[21] *Didache* 14:1 (see Apostolic Constitutions 7:30:1); Ignatius, Magnesians. 9:1; Gospel of Peter 35, 50. See R. J. Bauckham, "The Lord's Day" and "Sabbath and Sunday in the Post-Apostolic Church," in D. A. Carson, ed., *From Sabbath to Lord's Day: A Biblical, Historical and Theological Investigation* (Grand Rapids: Zondervan, 1982), 221–98.
[22] Rom 12:1.

you do, whether in word or deed, do it all in the name of
the Lord Jesus, giving thanks to God the Father through
him."[23] Worship of God is the supreme end of the Christian
church, whether considered locally or universally, or in the
individual lives of its members.

The Church as Means of Grace

In addition to looking up, the church exists in order to
look across. Put another way, the church's vertical purpose
to worship God mandates its horizontal purpose: working to
evangelize the lost and edify the church.

The church itself is a means of grace not because it
grants salvation apart from faith but because it is the God-
ordained means his Spirit uses to proclaim the saving gospel, to illustrate the gospel, and to confirm the gospel. The
church is the conduit through which the benefits of Christ's
death normally come.

Edification: Individual Discipleship and Growth

The purpose of the church, in part, is to encourage individual Christians in their faith and relationship with Christ.
With this goal in mind, Paul prayed that the Ephesian congregation "will in all things grow up into him who is the Head,
that is, Christ. From him the whole body, joined and held
together by every supporting ligament, grows and builds itself
up in love, as each part does its work."[24] When the author
of Hebrews exhorted his readers to assemble regularly, he
pointed to the purpose of giving mutual encouragement: "Let
us consider how we may spur one another on toward love and
good deeds. Let us not give up meeting together, as some are
in the habit of doing, but let us encourage one another."[25]

Edification: Constructing Community

The whole congregation's life together should aim at
corporate edification, an idea that has its roots in the Old

---

[23] Col 3:17; cf. 1 Cor 10:31.
[24] Eph 4:15–16.
[25] Heb 10:24–25.

Testament people of God. God created a people in the Old Testament to be specially blessed by his presence, promises, and power. His goal was for them to display his faithfulness to his promises, his character by following his laws, and his lordship by looking forward to the promised day of his coming. The nation was to be a people marked by holiness.

In the New Testament the people of God are the church. In a local congregation the fellowship as a whole is to display the holiness of God through its holiness. God's love is to be reflected in the love they show one another. The unity of God is to be reflected in their own unity.[26] The fellowship of believers in a congregation should be a partnership in laboring for mutual edification and for faithfulness in evangelism.

Evangelism

Another purpose of the local congregation is to bring God's Word to those outside the church.[27] Jesus commanded the disciples to "go and make disciples of all nations, baptizing them in the name of the Father and of the Son and of the Holy Spirit, and teaching them to obey everything I have commanded you."[28] He also told them that the forgiveness of sins would be preached in his name "beginning at Jerusalem."[29] "You will be my witnesses," Jesus said to them, "in Jerusalem, and in all Judea and Samaria, and to the ends of the earth" (Acts 1:8).

Opportunities for ministry to others naturally arise in the neighborhood and city where a congregation lives. The good news spreads most naturally not only where the congregation holds its assembly but where its scattered members live out their weekdays. Their lives should be known by non-Christian friends, neighbors, and colleagues. Their

---

[26] First Corinthians has all of these themes.
[27] "The mission of the church is to go into the world and make disciples by declaring the gospel of Jesus Christ in the power of the Spirit and gathering these disciples into churches, that they might worship the Lord and obey his commands now and in eternity to the glory of God the Father" (Kevin DeYoung and Greg Gilbert, *What Is the Mission of the Church?* [Wheaton, IL: Crossway, 2011], 62).
[28] Matt 28:19–20.
[29] Luke 24:47.

witness should be improved as all these outsiders constantly observe their conduct.

Missions

The outward purpose of the church is not limited to evangelizing a congregation's own city. A congregation's prayers and plans should stretch beyond the narrow horizons of familiarity. Jesus' command to go "to the ends of the earth" reminds believers that Christ is Lord over all, that he loves all, and that he will call all to account on the great day. Therefore, Christians today have a responsibility to take the gospel around the world. That responsibility lies not just with individual Christians but with congregations. Christians together can pool wisdom, experience, financial support, prayers, and callings and direct them all to the common purpose of making God's name great among the nations.

In many urban churches today, this outward purpose might require restructuring life so that members of the congregation naturally intersect with unbelieving populations in the metropolitan areas. In all churches this outward purpose means praying and planning to send resources and people to those people groups who have not yet heard the gospel of Jesus Christ. Witnessing the glory of God proclaimed around the globe in the hearts of all his people should be an end and purpose for every local church.

Always the Glory of God

The final, and most important, aspect of the church's purpose is the glory of God.

In the Old Testament, God created a people for the glory of his name.[30] Even when he saved them from the results of their own sin, he saved them for the glory of his own name. Speaking through Ezekiel, God said:

> It is not for your sake, O house of Israel, that I am going to do these things, but for the sake of my holy name, which you have profaned among the nations

---

[30] For example, see the Lord's reasoning for the plagues in Exodus 9–12.

where you have gone. I will show the holiness of my great name, which has been profaned among the nations, the name you have profaned among them. Then the nations will know that I am the LORD, declares the Sovereign LORD, when I show myself holy through you before their eyes.[31]

The same is true in the New Testament. The church ultimately exists for the glory of God. Whether pursuing missions or evangelism; edifying one another through prayer and Bible study; encouraging growth in holiness; or assembling for public praise, prayer, and instruction, this one purpose prevails. The church is the unique instrument for bringing God such glory. According to the Bible, God's "intent was that now, through the church, the manifold wisdom of God should be made known to the rulers and authorities in the heavenly realms, according to his eternal purpose which he accomplished in Christ Jesus our Lord."[32] No lesser matters are at stake in the church than the promulgation of God's glory throughout his creation. As Charles Bridges expressed it, "The Church is the mirror, that reflects the whole effulgence of the Divine character. It is the grand scene, in which the perfections of Jehovah are displayed to the universe."[33]

---

[31] Ezek 36:22–23; cf. Isa 48:8–11.

[32] Eph 3:10–11.

[33] Charles Bridges, *The Christian Ministry* (1830; repr. Edinburgh: Banner of Truth, 1980), 1. Cf. J. L. Reynolds's majestic statement: "When Christ uttered, in the judgment hall of Pilate, the remarkable words—'I am a king,' he pronounced a sentiment fraught with unspeakable dignity and power. His enemies might deride his pretensions and express their mockery of his claim, by presenting him with a crown of thorns, a reed and a purple robe, and nailing him to the cross; but in the eyes of unfallen intelligences, he was a king. A higher power presided over that derisive ceremony, and converted it into a real coronation. That crown of thorns was indeed the diadem of empire; that purple robe was the badge of royalty; that fragile reed was the symbol of unbounded power; and that cross the throne of dominion which shall never end" (J. L. Reynolds, "Church Polity, of the Kingdom of Christ," in *Polity: Biblical Arguments on How to Conduct Church Life*, ed. Mark Dever [Washington, DC: Center for Church Reform, 2001], 298). "It is as though the church is a stage upon which God has been presenting the great drama of redemption, a true-life pageant in which it is shown how those who have rebelled against God and wrecked his universe are now being brought back into harmony with him, becoming agents of renewing and healing instead" (James Montgomery Boice, *Foundations of the Christian Faith* [rev. ed., Downers Grove: IVP, 1986], 565–66).

8

The Hope of the Church

The Gospel and Justice

Two principles clarify the relationship between the church and matters of social justice. First, the activities of the collective and institutional local church should be viewed distinctly from the activities of the church's individual members as they disperse to fulfill their various roles in life. Second, the church's activity must be understood in light of the church's hope.

The Bible calls individual Christians to live lives of justice and generosity toward others. Organically, Christian disciples scatter and represent Christ powerfully and in ways the Bible does not call the institutional church to act. An analogy might be helpful here. A married man goes to work as a married man and goes to the store as a married man, and the fact that he's married affects how he interacts with others at work and the store, but neither his work nor shopping are an intrinsic part of being married. In the same way, a member of a church follows Christ in all sorts of ways that are not tied to the work that God entrusts to the local church in any institutional fashion. But the individual's membership should affect how he does everything outside the gathered church.

Individually, people are made for God and are to be devoted to him supremely. Christians should have hearts of compassion for all people, not merely because they are part of creation but especially because they are made in God's image (Prov 14:31) and because we ourselves have known such undeserved generosity from God (Luke 6:32–36; 2 Cor 8:8–9; Jas 2:13). It is a privilege to serve any human being. And it is a joy to reflect God's own just character (Isa 1:17; Dan 4:27) as well as the sacrificial love of Christ. In this sense ministries of compassion and justice are wonderful signs of Christ's giving himself for us in the gospel.

In other words, Christians should desire to see non-Christians know the common blessings of God's kindness in providence (e.g., food, water, family relations, jobs, good government, justice). It is therefore both appropriate and wise for Christians and congregations to take action to this end. Furthermore, the temporary institutions of this world (like marriage) are worthy of sincere Christian attention, thought, energy, and action. Christian teaching must not platonically devalue this world. Instead, Christians are called to do all things unto the Lord (see Col 3:17). Paul in Romans 9–10 is a model of Christian aspirations for the eternal good of non-Christians.

At the same time Christ gave the church a unique institutional mandate to preach, display, model, and express the good news of Jesus Christ.[1] And in obedience to *that* institutional mandate, Christian congregations have both the liberty and the responsibility to take prudent initiatives in advocating mercy or justice in our community as opportunities arise, perhaps collectively in the name of the church and certainly as individuals in the name of Christ.[2]

---

[1] James Bannerman carefully distinguished the local church from the individual believer (James Bannerman, *The Church of Christ*, vol. 1 [repr., Edinburgh: Banner of Truth, 1960], 3).

[2] Acts 1:8; Gal 6:10. Protestant pastors and theologians like Jonathan Edwards and C. H. Spurgeon have referred in a general fashion to the "spirituality of the church." When used by these authors, the phrase is roughly equivalent to the purity and holiness of the church. But the phrase has also been given a more technical meaning in the context of conversations about political establishment and compromise, particularly among southern Presbyterians like J. H. Thornwell and R. L. Dabney. Here the phrase "spirituality of the church" refers to the need for keeping the

What all this means is that congregations *may* take
action in the cause of this-worldly justice, but they are not
required to. Certainly Christians are called to live lives of
love toward others. And Scripture in no way *denies* the right
or ability of a congregation to care for the physical needs of
non-Christians in its area. But neither does Scripture *require*

---

proper concerns of the church in focus and eschewing worldliness. For instance,
the church should not concern itself with affairs of the state, say advocates of the
spirituality of the church. And it should guard its own purity by its own authority,
rather than asking the state to protect it (see R. L. Dabney, *Lectures in Theology*,
4th ed. [Richmond: Presb. Committee of Publication, 1890], 873–87). After all,
advocates of "the spirituality of the church" drew a connection between the distinct
authorities of church and state and the distinct focuses of church and state. "The
church is to teach men the way to heaven and to help them thither. The state is to
protect each citizen in the enjoyment of temporal rights. The church has no civil
pains and penalties at command; because Christ has given her none and because
they have no relevancy whatever to produce her object—the hearty belief of saving truth. (See John 18:36; 2 Cor 10:4)" (Dabney, *Lectures in Theology*, 874–75).
Two crucial proponents of the doctrine were Stuart Robinson, *The Church of God*
(Philadelphia: Joseph M. Wilson, 1858), esp. 84–93, and Thomas E. Peck, *Notes on
Ecclesiology* (Richmond: Presbyterian Committee of Publication, 1893), esp. 119–
55. Against the idea that this was a solely southern doctrine, see Charles Hodges's
comments on the floor of the 1861 General Assembly of the Presbyterian Church:
"The doctrine of our church on this subject is, that the state has no authority in
matters purely spiritual and that the church has no authority in matters purely
secular or civil. That their provinces in some cases overlie each other . . . is indeed
true. . . . Nevertheless, the two institutions are distinct, and their respective duties
are different" ("The General Assembly," *Biblical Repertory and Princeton Review*
33 [1861], 557; see 561); cf. J. H. Thornwell, *Collected Writings of James Henley
Thornwell*, vol. 4 (1875; repr. Edinburgh: Banner of Truth Trust, 1974), 448–51;
B. M. Palmer, *Life and Letters of James Henley Thornwell* (1875; repr. Edinburgh:
Banner of Truth Trust, 1974), 501. Similar to Abraham Kuyper's "sphere sover-
eignty" ideas, the spirituality of the church in this more refined usage restricts the
church's concerns to matters of the gospel and issues directly related to the gospel.
Cf. Calvin, *Institutes,* II.xv.3–4; IV.xx.1. Other matters (like a concern for education, politics, and mercy ministries for nonchurch members) are proper concerns
for Christians to have, but the church itself is not the structure for addressing
such concerns. They are the proper concern of Christians in schools, governments,
and other structures of society. In fact, if such concerns came to be the focus of
the church, they could potentially distract the church from its main and unique
responsibility, that of living out and proclaiming the gospel. A helpful summary
of this nineteenth-century discussion can be found in Daryl G. Hart, *Recovering
Mother Kirk* (Grand Rapids: Baker, 2003), 51–65; David VanDrunen, *Natural Law
and the Two Kingdoms: A Study in the Development of Reformed Social Thought*
(Grand Rapids: Eerdmans, 2010), 247–67; cf. Preston D. Graham Jr., *A Kingdom
Not of This World: Stuart Robinson's Struggle to Distinguish the Sacred from the
Secular During the Civil War* (Macon, GA: Mercer University Press, 2002). For a
contemporary treatment of at least the implications of this, see Brian Habig and
Les Newsom, *The Enduring Community: Embracing the Priority of the Church*
(Jackson, MS: Reformed University Press, 2001).

the local congregation to organize as a whole to alleviate the physical needs of non-Christians in the community.[3]

Each local church has the freedom to choose particular actions for serving the welfare of its community in order to witness to the community directly, or a church is free to do this more remotely by cooperating with other congregations and Christians by forming denominations, educational institutions, and a great variety of boards, charities, and other organizations.

Churches should teach and pray for and expect their members to be involved in a wide variety of good works,[4] some of which may be held up as examples to other members. This can be done without leading the congregation as a whole to own or support those particular ministries (by congregationally funding or staffing them). Pastors and church leaders can personally set an example of care for others.[5]

At the same time, social action or "mercy ministries" (e.g., soup kitchens, medical clinics, etc.) must never be mistaken for evangelism. They may be a means to evangelism, but they are not evangelism. The church's main responsibility is gospel proclamation.[6] Nothing must obscure the church's central obligation to preach the gospel. Expounding Scripture in the local church equips members to understand and express God's character of justice and mercy appropriately to the world. And this rightly means touching on issues

---

[3] The gospel is, properly speaking, preached, not done (though the individual's actions can certainly affirm it; see John 13:34–35 [even here Christian love for *one another* points to the gospel!]). Social ministry done by the church should be self-consciously engaged in with the hope, prayer, and design of sharing the gospel. J. Gresham Machen wrote that "material benefits were never valued in the apostolic age for their own sake, they were never regarded as substitutes for spiritual things. That lesson needs to be learned. Social betterment, though important, is insufficient; it must always be supplemented by God's unspeakable gift" (J. Gresham Machen, ed. John Cook, *New Testament*, 345–46).

[4] See Prov 19:17; 21:3; Luke 10:25–37; Acts 9:36; Heb 13:1–3; Jas 1:27.

[5] So John Wesley "began the year 1785, by spending five days walking through London, often ankle deep in sludge and melting snow, to beg 200 pounds, which he employed in purchasing clothing for the poor. He visited the destitute in their own houses, 'to see with his own eyes what their wants were, and how they might be effectually relieved.'" Wesley was 81 years old! (L. Tyerman, *Life and Times of Wesley* [New York: Harper & Bros., 1872], III.458).

[6] "Evangelism is the most basic and radical ministry possible to a human being" (Tim Keller, "The Gospel and the Poor," *Themelios* 33, no. 3 [December 2008]: 17).

of poverty, gender, racism, and justice from the pulpit.[7] Such teaching, however, should normally occur without committing the church to particular public policy solutions. For example, Christian preachers could strenuously advocate the abolition of human trafficking without laying out specific policy proposals for how to do it. Christian preaching can speak to what ought to be done without assuming it has the expertise to untangle all the means necessary for achieving those good ends.

A non-Christian's greatest need is to hear the gospel. The proclamation of the gospel addresses the greatest part of human suffering caused by the fall. It is central to fulfilling the Great Commission (Matt 28:18–20). And it is central to fulfilling the great commandments (Mark 12:29–31; cf. Gal 6:2). For the Christian these commandments must lie at the heart of any cultural mandate (Gen 1:28).[8]

What is the church's ministry to the world? It may be important first to consider what it is not. The Christian congregation is not required to take institutional responsibility for the physical needs in the unbelieving community.[9] The Scriptures do make Christians responsible to care for the needs of the members of their own churches,[10] though even here the New Testament makes further qualifications.[11] Paul's instructions to Timothy concerning the care of widows seems to indicate the church was to care for *Christian*

[7] Consider God's concerns evidenced in Isa 1:10–17. God cares about the ethical behavior of those who are not his special covenant people. Christian churches in prosperous areas should warn their congregations about the dangers of accumulating wealth. Many Christians throughout history have read the Bible as being more suspicious of wealth than Christians in modern America seem to be. Everyone from Augustine to Wesley has written eloquently of the dangerous gravity of wealth and the worldly pull it can have on Christians. Such teaching need not be opposed to careful financial planning, but it should cause more vigilance, more wariness, and even suspicion of wealth. Fresh attention should be given to cautionary passages like Matt 6:21; Luke 12:34; 1 Tim 6:17–19; and Jas 5:1–6. According to the Bible, wealth can be more spiritually dangerous than poverty.
[8] Note the cultural advances that were in the line of Cain—building a city, raising livestock, music, metalworking (see Gen 4:17,20–22).
[9] Many texts which seem to promote the idea of taking responsibility for our community's physical well-being (e.g., Mic 6:8, Matthew 25; Galatians 6; 1 John 3) are about our charity to members of the covenant community—believers, not non-Christian members of the community at large.
[10] Matt 25:34–40; Acts 6:1–6; Gal 6:2,10; Jas 2:15–16; 1 John 3:17–19.
[11] For example, 2 Thess 3:10; 1 Tim 5:3–16.

widows (1 Tim 5:3–16). Yet such care was to be given only
when there was a lack of family support. Paul instructed family members to care for their own needy first, if at all possible
(v. 16). By the same token, we might conclude that support
that can be acquired from outside the church (for instance,
from the state) should be preferred over using church funds,
thus freeing church funds to be used elsewhere.

In summary, congregations must carefully prioritize
the responsibilities unique to the church. It is proper for
Christians to be concerned with education, politics, and
mercy ministry, but the church itself is not the structure
established by God for addressing such concerns. Such matters are the proper concern of Christians in schools, governments, and other structures of society. In fact, churches
must be careful not to let such concerns distract them from
their main and unique responsibility, that of embodying and
proclaiming the gospel. John Murray put it well:

> To the church is committed the task of proclaiming
> the whole counsel of God and, therefore, the coun-
> sel of God as it bears upon the responsibility of all
> persons and institutions. While the church is not to
> discharge the functions of other institutions such as
> the state and the family, nevertheless it is charged to
> define what the functions of these institutions are.[12]

Local church leaders should therefore be careful to
protect the practice and priority of evangelism in the life of
the local church. Furthermore, leaders should protect the
church from being divided unnecessarily over issues that are
not essential for a local church to agree on (e.g., nuclear
disarmament, constitutional amendments, art outreaches,
or various kinds of ministries in the community).

The Consummation

Suffering is an inevitable part of this fallen world. Poverty,
war, famine, death, and other tragic effects of the fall will not

[12] John Murray, "The Relation of Church and State," in *Collected Writings of John Murray*, vol. 1 (Banner of Truth, 1976), 255.

end except by the bodily, visible return of Christ (see Mark 14:7; John 12:8; Rev 6:1–11). The heavenly city will come down; it won't be built up, constructed from the ground up, as it were (Heb 11:10; Rev 21:2). Its coming is as one-sided as creation, the exodus, the incarnation, the crucifixion, the resurrection, and the regeneration of the individual heart. It is a great salvation act of God. If human culture can ever be said to be redeemed, it will be God doing it, not us.

The gospel's main thrust is not to renew the fallen structures of this world but rather to create a new community of those purchased by the blood of the Lamb (Rev 5:6–12) and washed with his Word (Eph 5:26–27). Only through the fulfillment of God's promise to forgive sin are all of God's other promises fulfilled. The joy of being reconciled to God and the prospect of being in his presence is superior to all the goods of this world. No gospel that describes Scripture's sweeping narrative as culminating in the coming of the kingdom but neglects to explain how individuals can be included in that kingdom is any true gospel.

Scripture presents no hope that society will be broadly and permanently transformed by the preaching of the gospel (see Matt 24:21–22,29), which is not to deny that great good will be done through the church's faithful stewardship of the gospel. Individual conversions will have profound effects for good on people, not only in eternity but in this life. Studies suggest that conservative evangelicals tend to give more to the poor than religious liberals.[13] Certainly, many individual

---

[13] See Robert Wuthnow, *Acts of Compassion* (Princeton, NJ: Princeton University Press, 1993). Though John Wesley lamented the temptation of wealth, he gave eloquent testimony to the power of the gospel to practically improve someone's life. He observed in 1787 that "I fear, wherever riches have increased . . . the essence of religion, the mind that was in Christ, has decreased in the same proportion. Therefore, I do not see how it is possible, in the nature of things, for any revival of true religion to continue long. For religion must necessarily produce both industry and frugality; and these cannot but produce riches. But as riches increase, so will pride, anger, and love of the world in all its branches. How then is it possible that Methodism, that is, the religion of the heart, though it flourishes now as a green bay tree, should continue in this state? For the Methodists in every place grow diligent and frugal; consequently they increase in goods. Hence, they proportionably increase in pride, in the desire of the flesh, the desire of the eyes, and the pride of life. So, although the form of religion remains, the spirit is swiftly vanishing away. Is there no way to prevent this? this continual declension of pure religion? We ought not to forbid people to be diligent and frugal; we *must* exhort all Christians,

conversions have resulted in personal reformations and
particular social improvements.[14] But the church is called
to herald no vision of a this-world utopia. The trajectory
of unredeemed human history as recorded in the Bible is
always *toward* judgment. Consider the flood, Babel, Canaan,
Egypt, Jerusalem, Babylon, Rome, and the final judgment
depicted in Revelation 19.

The heavenly city in Scripture, though bearing some
continuity with our own age (perhaps Rev 21:24), is presented as arriving only after a radical disjunction with our
current history, including the judgment of the wicked.[15] The
material world is to be restored only after going through a
change as significant as death (2 Pet 3:7). This is why Jesus
told Pilate, "My kingdom is not of this world. . . . But now
my kingdom is from another place" (John 18:36). Christ's
kingdom will come to this place (Acts 1:6–8), though when
he comes, he will renew this place (Rom 8:21).

In the Bible, God's people are given great hope. God's
people begin in a garden (Genesis 2–3) but end in a city
(Revelation 21–22). The garden is Eden, and God created it
to be the perfect environment for those made in his image.
It had everything humans would need, from food to work to
companionship. Most of all, the garden enjoyed God's own
presence, and God enjoyed unbroken fellowship with his
people in the garden.

Sin destroyed the fellowship between God, man, and creation. But the destruction made way for an even grander display of God's glory in the church. In another garden Christ
faced Adam's choice—to follow his own will or the will of
his heavenly Father. In God's mercy and grace, Christ, the
second Adam, chose to follow God's will and to take him at

---

to gain all they can, and to save all they can: this is, in effect, to grow rich! What way
then, I ask again, can we take that our money may not sink us to the nethermost
hell? There is one way, and there is no other under heaven. If those who *gain all
they can*, and *save all they can*, will likewise *give all they can*, then the more they
gain, the more they will grow in grace, and the more treasure they will lay up in
heaven" (Tyerman, vol. III, 520).

[14] See *Journal for the Scientific Study of Religion* 37, no. 3 (September 1998); also
Robert Wuthnow's *Acts of Compassion*.

[15] See Ps 102:26; Isa 13:10; 34:4; 51:6,16; 65:17; 66:22; Matt 5:18; 24:29,35; 1 Cor
7:31; 2 Pet 3:10–13; 1 John 2:17; Rev 6:12–14; 21:1.

his word. What followed was the most terrible suffering by the only person ever undeserving of such suffering. Then, after he had borne the sins of his people as a substitute, and after he had exhausted the claims of God's wrath against them, Christ was raised in victory over sin and death. He then poured out his Spirit and created his church.

From there, God's people have spread around the world to share the good news of Jesus Christ. The mission of the church will succeed. Jesus promised his disciples that the gates of Hades would not prevail against his church (Matt 16:18). Christians may wonder at God's patience with the church and fear for our own poor stewardship of the church, but we cannot be anything other than confident about the church. It will succeed.[16] The church is God's plan and purpose.

The culmination of history is pictured in the end of Revelation as a heavenly city, an eternal society of light in which God himself is personally present. The fellowship of Eden has been restored. Only this time the number of inhabitants has been multiplied many millions of times over, as has the intimacy of fellowship since God's own Spirit inhabits all those who trust in Christ alone for the forgiveness of their sins. The garden has become the city. Faith gives way to sight. God's glory is magnified as the eternal love between the three persons of the Trinity is reflected forever in the interpersonal love shared between the bride and the groom, the church and Christ.

Christ's prayer for his disciples in John 17:26 will then be fully answered: "I have made you known to them, and will continue to make you known in order that the love you have for me may be in them and that I myself may be in them." In the heavenly city Christians will enter fully and eternally into the love of God. The church on earth today presents the glimmering and growing picture of this coming reality.

---

[16] Eph 2:10; 1 Thess 5:24.

Part 2

What Has the Church Believed?

9

The History of the
Idea of the Church

The topic of the church itself has been of intermittent interest in the history of the church. In the fourth century the church's intense struggle with the Donatists was a controversy that focused significantly on the nature of the church. In the Middle Ages the struggle over the bishop of Rome's authority helped separate East and West, and it caused great struggles among theologians in the West. Later, Jan Hus, John Wycliffe, and other medieval non-conformists pressed a doctrine of the invisible church in which Christ, not the pope, was head. What follows are some important questions that arose out of these controversies.

Important Dichotomies

Visible or Invisible?

The assemblies of Christians, or local churches, mentioned in the New Testament are examples of visible churches. God has designed the church to be an apparent and visible testimony of him to the watching world. But is *visible* the only way the church can be described? After all, Jesus stated that weeds have been sown among the wheat but that the two will be separated on the last day (Matt 13:20–23). We can also speak of the *invisible* church, that is, the church as God sees it, or as it will appear on the last day. The invisible church is the church composed of all true believers, whether or not they are in the visible church, and excluding those in the visible church who are not genuinely converted.

Historically, Protestants have championed the distinction between the invisible and visible church. This distinction has been used to explain the absence of the visible unity for which Christ prayed in John 17. By its nature the invisible church is united; the visible church is sadly mixed and divided. While it is not accurate to say that the idea of the invisible church began with the Protestant Reformation, since the idea is found in Wycliffe, Hus, and even Augustine, the Protestant Reformers made particular use of the idea.[1] There are not two separate churches, one visible and one invisible; these are two aspects of the true church.[2]

Local or Universal?

Another dichotomy with a significant history of theological consideration in the church has been the distinction made between the *local church* and the *universal church* or (catholic church). That church which is composed of all Christians throughout history is the universal church.[3] While the universal church has never assembled, one day it will, and Christians currently are regarded by God as a part of that elect body. On the other hand, the local church is simply the local assembly of Christians. With one possible exception (Luke's interesting use in Acts 9:31), the word *church* in the New Testament always refers either to a local assembly (the great majority of usages) or to the universal

---

[1] John Calvin, *Institutes*, IV.1.7; cf. Benjamin Keach's catechism, Questions 105–6, reprinted in Tom J. Nettles, *Teaching Truth, Training Hearts* (Amityville, NY: Calvary, 1998).

[2] "This Church is said to be invisible, because she is essentially spiritual and in her spiritual essence cannot be discerned by the physical eye; and because it is impossible to determine infallibly who do and who do not belong to her" (Berkhof, *Systematic Theology*, 566–67); cf. Westminster Confession, chap. 25.

[3] E.g., Jesus in Matt 16:18 was referring not to one local church but to the one universal church as "my church."

church (a handful of usages).[4] Christians have historically accepted that both of these usages are found in the New Testament. Two significant disputes, however, have raged concerning this dichotomy.

First, and most significant for the church around the world, has been the dispute about whether there is a prescribed order and polity for the universal church, as there is for the local church. The Roman Catholic Church maintains a universal order exists. The Greek Orthodox and many Protestant groups maintain that structures have developed which are allowed and useful though not mandated in Scripture (e.g., national assemblies, conventions, archbishops, etc.). On the other hand, congregationalists, like Baptists, have maintained that the New Testament prescribes no structure for the universal church. All cooperation between congregations is understood to be voluntary and consensual.

A second controversy of particular concern to Baptist Christians has surrounded the question of whether one can legitimately refer to something as a church if an order or structure for it has not been set down in Scripture. Ironically, some nineteenth-century Baptists and their heirs agree with this aspect of Roman Catholic thought—that the invisible church does not exist apart from a divinely given visible structure. However, they join this to the conclusion that the universal church is never discussed in the New Testament. This controversy was known as "Landmarkism," named after Prov 22:28: "remove not the ancient landmark which your fathers have set" (KJV). This was the text for a sermon by J. M. Pendleton and the basis of J. R. Graves's book, *Old Landmarkism: What Is It?* (1854). This book became a manifesto for the movement and exercised great influence among Baptists in certain parts of the United States.[5]

---

[4] On Acts 9:31, see F. F. Bruce's comments, in Bruce, *Acts* in NICNT, ed. F. F. Bruce (Grand Rapids: Eerdmans, 1983), 208–9; cf. A. H. Strong, *Systematic Theology* (Valley Forge: Judson, 1907), 891.

[5] One can get something of an idea of the seriousness of the controversy when it is noted that Basil Manly Jr.'s 1859 "Abstract of Principles," written for The Southern Baptist Theological Seminary, lacks any affirmation of the existence of the universal church—a matter which would have been uncontroversial among Baptists two

Militant or Triumphant?

Still another dichotomy which has been used to describe different aspects of the church is the *church militant* and the *church triumphant*.[6] The church militant refers to Christians alive now, who therefore remain engaged in battling the world, the flesh, and the devil.[7] The church triumphant, however, refers to Christians now in heaven, removed from the combat of spiritual warfare and fully victorious.[8] The Roman Catholic Church also speaks of the *church suffering*, by which they mean both the church now on earth as well as those who are redeemed but are still being purified in purgatory.

True or False?

The topic of the church became the focal point of formal theological debate in the Reformation. Here, as in so much of the church's theological development, the question of how to distinguish the *true* from the *false* led to a clearer definition of the true.

Before the sixteenth century the church was more assumed than discussed. It was regarded as a means of grace, a reality that existed, and a presupposition for the rest of theology. Roman Catholic theology commonly refers to "the mystery of the church," by which it means the inexhaustible, imponderable depth of this reality of the church. Thus, in the Vulgate, Eph 5:32 refers to the union of Christ with his church as a "sacramentum" or mystery. Practically, the church of Rome argued that it was the true, visible church according to Petrine succession through the bishop of Rome [pope], based on Jesus' words to Peter in Matt 16:17–19.

---

or three decades earlier. For a careful consideration of the exegetical and theological claims of Landmarkism, see John Thornbury, *The Doctrine of the Church: A Baptist View* (Pasadena, TX: Pilgrim Publications, 1971) and James A. Patterson, *James Robinson Graves: Staking the Boundaries of Baptist Identity* (Nashville: B&H, 2012).

[6] Such language can be found in Aquinas and in Wycliffe.

[7] See the classic Puritan treatment of the militant nature of the church's life in this world by William Gurnall, *The Christian in Complete Armor* (1662–65; repr. Edinburgh: Banner of Truth, 1964).

[8] See Berkhof, *Systematic Theology*, 565.

With the advent of the Reformation, discussion of the church's nature became inevitable. To the Protestant reformers, "Not the pretended chair of Peter, but the teaching of Peter was the real mark of apostolicity. The Reformation made the gospel, not ecclesiastical organization, the test of the true church."[9] Calvin criticized Rome's claims to be a true church on the basis of apostolic succession: "Especially in the organization of the church nothing is more absurd than to lodge the succession in persons alone to the exclusion of teaching."[10] Believing that the attributes of the church (one, holy, universal, and apostolic) had become insufficient to distinguish between a true and a false church, the Reformation introduced the *notae ecclesiae,* the marks of the church: the right preaching of God's Word and the right administration of the ordinances.

Beginning with the Reformation, then, Protestants have believed that an individual, local congregation should be regarded as a true church when the Word of God is rightly preached and the ordinances of Christ are rightly followed.[11] The right preaching of the Word of God is the *formative discipline* which shapes the church (as opposed to *corrective discipline*, which includes measures like excommunication). The ministry of the Word, therefore, is central and defining. The way to distinguish between a true church and a false church is to ask whether the church's public worship consists of right preaching of God's Word and the right administration of the ordinances. If both are present, a true church has been found.[12] The Word being rightly taught should lead the church to rightly administer the ordinances of Christ (which would also imply discipline being exercised).[13]

---

[9] Clowney, *The Church*, 101.
[10] Calvin, *Institutes*, IV.ii.3; cf. the 1536 edition in II.29.
[11] Examples of this can be found in Iain Murray, ed., *Documents for the Reformation of the Church* (Edinburgh: Banner of Truth, 1965), 15–23.
[12] It should be noted that true churches can be divided between those true churches that are regular and those that are irregular, that is, between those that are according to the rule (*regula*) and those that are not. Thus, various Protestant churches may recognize one another as true churches but irregular (depending on their differences on matters such as polity and the proper subjects or mode of baptism).
[13] This understanding of the nature of the true church led to changes in physical church structures, changes in the service (more time for congregational singing,

Unity of the Church (Organizational or Organic?)

Closely related to the idea of the church's universality is the idea of the church's unity. In the early church Christians presented their unity as a bulwark against heretics and schismatics. But mutual excommunications over issues like Nestorianism, monophysitism, or papal supremacy rent the visible unity of the church. The church was further divided during the Reformation both by the Protestant understanding of the gospel and by their method of understanding that gospel—through the clear (perspicuous) and sufficient Scriptures rather than the mediation of the church. Roman Catholics have insisted on a visible unity of the church. Protestants have insisted instead on the primacy of a unity in doctrine and spirit.

Rise of Denominations

Denominations, as they are known today, arose largely in the seventeenth century, though their roots are earlier. Protestants did not look upon dividing the visible church lightly, but the Protestant principles of Scripture's perspicuity and authority gave them warrant, or even required them, to divide from false teaching. As Calvin said, "We acknowledge no unity except in Christ; no charity of which he is not the bond; and . . . therefore, the chief point in preserving charity is to maintain Faith sacred and entire."[14] This meant that the Reformers recognized that the cost of unity at the price of truth was a bad bargain. Correct division should be preferred over corrupt unity. For these reasons various groups on the European continent struggled free from the control of established churches and began pursuing their own understanding of faithfulness to Scripture.

Most of the denominations popularly known in America today initially grew up in the United Kingdom. Presbyterianism, congregationalism, and a belief in believer's

---

for the sermon), and changes in the minister's role. He changed from being a priest offering sacrifices to being a minister of the Word and a pastor of the people.

[14] John Calvin, in his preface to *Psychopannychia*, in *Selected Works of John Calvin: Tracts and Letters*, vol. 3, ed. and trans. Henry Beveridge and Jules Bonnet (1851; repr., Grand Rapids: Baker, 1983), 416.

baptism are all derived from Queen Elizabeth I's England (1558–1603). However, the English government did not tolerate any congregations outside the established church until the late seventeenth century, almost 100 years later. Denominations may have solidified divisions in the church, but they also eased the pinched consciences of many careful Christians in the seventeenth century. Freedom to meet together and to worship according to one's conscience was a fundamental step in the development of denominations as they are known today.

The three "old denominations," as they were called, were the Presbyterians, the Congregationalists, and the Baptists. These three joined the establishment Episcopalians and the eighteenth-century denomination, the Methodists, to comprise the British-born religious landscape of early America. Once other significant ethnic groups were added, such as the Dutch and French Reformed churches or the German and Scandinavian Lutheran groups, America became the primary laboratory for scores of denominations of Christian churches coexisting.

These groupings of churches largely retained their doctrinal and practical distinctives, and new ones have emerged since then. Many families of churches arise from a struggle for purity. This was true in England in the sixteenth and seventeenth centuries. As questions of the gospel were settled, secondary but important issues of church government and discipline led to separate congregations of Baptists, Congregationalists, and Presbyterians. Advocates and opponents of slavery divided major denominations. Numerous divisions among heirs of Wesley and doctrinal disagreements among Presbyterians added to the denominational divisions of the nineteenth century. The rise of modern religious unbelief in mainline Protestant denominations in early twentieth-century America led to another burst of congregations and denominations separating from older groups and formed new, purer groups.[15]

---

[15] For a classic text explaining and advocating this idea of "biblical separation," see Ernest Pickering, *Biblical Separation: The Struggle for a Pure Church* (Schaumburg, IL; Regular Baptist Press, 1979). Two instructive critiques of

Both the doctrinal convictions themselves and the importance attached to them have proved to be grounds for both unity and division among Christians. In short, the rise of differing denominations represents the desire for faithfulness in purity rather than in visible unity.[16] Every congregation decides which beliefs and practices members must share before they can in good conscience experience and express unity with them.

evangelicalism over just these points are Iain H. Murray, *Evangelicalism Divided: A Record of the Crucial Change in the Years 1950 to 2000* (Edinburgh: Banner of Truth, 2000); and Rolland McCune, *Promise Unfulfilled: The Failed Strategy of Modern Evangelicalism* (Greenville, SC: Ambassador International, 2004). For an Anglican perspective on some of these same themes, see Michael B. Thompson, *When Should We Divide?* (Cambridge, UK: Grove Books, 2004).

[16] "For the New Testament unity is in order to preserve the faith, not something which can exist irrespective of doctrinal purity" (Iain Murray, *Evangelicalism Divided* [Edinburgh: Banner of Truth Trust, 2000], 140).

10

The History of the
Ordinances of the Church

Which Ordinances?

It is sadly ironic that the actions Christians are commanded to share commonly—acknowledge "one baptism" (Eph 4:5) and celebrate the Lord's Supper together (1 Cor 11:18,21,33)—have been the focus of much dispute and division through the church's history. Disputes have centered on both the number and the nature of the ordinances to be practiced by the church.

Roman Catholic Church

Among theologians between Augustine in the fifth century and Hugo of St. Victor in the twelfth century, there was not an agreed-on number of sacraments.[1] Numbers ranged from two all the way to 30 or more. Since the thirteenth century the Roman Catholic Church has acknowledged seven sacraments. The theologians of the twelfth and thirteenth centuries, especially Hugo of St. Victor, Peter Lombard, Alexander of Hales, and Thomas Aquinas, largely brought the Roman Church to its current understanding of the number

---

[1] Eastern Orthodox churches today are still less uniform in establishing a specific number of sacraments.

and nature of the sacraments. Along with baptism and the Eucharist, the Roman Catholic Church also teaches that confirmation, confession and penance, marriage, ordination to the priesthood, and extreme unction (last rites) are sacraments to be observed by Christians as God's ordained means of grace.

While arguments might be made for the biblical basis of these latter five, the Roman Catholic Church does not hold to the sufficiency of Scripture. Instead, it teaches that the traditions of the Church, along with Scripture, preserve God's revealed will for his people. Therefore, the development of any of these sacraments after the New Testament writings is, in and of itself, no embarrassment to Roman Catholic theology.

Quakers and Salvationists

Other groups, such as the Quakers and the Salvation Army, have maintained that no ritual ordinances should be observed today, not even baptism and the Lord's Supper. They teach that these actions were meant for the first believers only and were never intended as continuing observances for the church. What must continue, however, are the spiritual realities of descending into new life in Christ and communing with God who has now come. Both of these things were signified by baptism and the Lord's Supper.

Speaking about George Fox, founder of the Quakers, Rufus Jones wrote:

> His house of worship was bare of everything but seats. It had no shrine, for the *shekinah* was to be in the hearts of those who worshipped. It had no altar, for God needed no appeasing, seeing that he himself had made the sacrifice for sin. It had no baptismal font, for baptism was in his belief nothing short of immersion into the life of the Father, Son and Holy Spirit—a going down into the significance of Christ's death and a coming up in newness of life with him. There was no communion table, because he believed that the true communion consisted in partaking

directly of the soul's spiritual bread—the living Christ.[2]

Certainly, Fox's eschewal of baptism and communion is consistent with his prioritization of the Inner Light (taken from John 1:9) over and above the written Word of God.

Some Baptists: Foot-Washing

Some Christians have maintained that foot-washing should be regarded as a third ordinance. Among these are a number of Old Regular and Regular Baptists, Primitive Baptists, Grace Brethren, and a few other groups.[3] Citing evidence from John 13:13–15, they construe Jesus' example not just as a lesson about humility; instead, they have taken this to mean Jesus intended the ritual to be continued by Christians. No historical records suggest that the early Christians practiced foot-washing as a church ordinance. Still, several of these groups in the post-Reformation period have reinitiated the practice.

Contemporary Evangelical Indifference

All the discussion concerning the number and nature of Christ's ordinances might seem far removed from the concerns of evangelical churches today. Christ's command to baptize is either ignored or minimized in the teaching of many churches, in the books written and read by evangelicals generally, and in the membership requirements of those churches. Also, the Lord's Supper is seldom celebrated in many congregations. Through all of this the Reformation doctrine *sola fide* ("faith alone") has been exploited for ill purposes, being used to relegate anything not directly necessary for salvation to the status of unimportant. But surely if Christ has commanded something, his followers have no authority to alter his command—either by adding to it or by ignoring it.

---

[2] Rufus Jones, "Introduction," to *George Fox, An Autobiography*, ed. R. Jones (London: Headley Bros., 1904), 22.
[3] See H. Dorgan, "Foot-Washing, Baptist Practice of," in *Dictionary of Baptists in America*, ed. Bill J. Leonard (Downers Grove: IVP, 1994), 119–20.

Baptism

Historically, Baptists were never in danger of ignoring Christ's ordinances. From name to practice, Baptists have been shaped by a particular understanding of baptism. Yet it has never been the practice of baptizing professing believers which has prompted controversy between different denominations. Rather, the baptism of infants has caused many of the debates and divisions in the history of Christian churches.

The Rise and Development of Infant Baptism

Considerable debate has raged around the question of when infant baptism was first practiced.[4] Proponents of infant baptism argue that first-century Christians performed infant baptism, though they must admit the New Testament evidence is inferential. Others have been less apt to find its origins in the earliest history of the church. From William Wall's *History of Infant Baptism*, the monumental seventeenth-century Anglican defense of the antiquity of infant baptism, to the famous mid-twentieth-century debate between New Testament scholars Joachim Jeremias and Kurt Aland, consensus has continued to elude scholars.[5] The *Didache, Letter of Barnabas,* and *The Shepherd of Hermas*, second-century documents that all reflect church

---

[4] One of the most careful and balanced treatments of the historical origin and development of infant baptism is David F. Wright, *Infant Baptism in Historical Perspective: Collected Studies* (Carlisle, UK: Paternoster, 2007). For a compilation and commentary on many of the earliest written records of infant baptism, see Hendrick Stander and Johannes Louw, *Baptism in the Early Church* (Leeds, England: Reformation Today Trust, 2004).

[5] William Wall (1647–1728), *The History of Infant Baptism* (London: J. Downing et al., 1705). Joachim Jeremias, *Infant Baptism in the First Four Centuries*, trans. David Cairns (London: SCM Press, 1960). Michael Horton stated that "by the second century the literature is replete with references to the practice [of infant baptism]" (Horton, *The Christian Faith* [Grand Rapids: Zondervan, 2011], 797). The present author has seen no convincing evidence of this assertion. See also Kurt Aland, *Did the Early Church Baptize Infants?* trans. G. R. Beasley-Murray (London: SCM Press, 1961); contra Aland, Joachim Jeremias, *The Origins of Infant Baptism: A Further Reply to Kurt Aland* (Naperville: A. R. Allenson, 1963). Aland held the interesting position that infants today should be baptized, even though, he admitted, no evidence exists for infant baptism before the third century. For a careful consideration of the evidence from the first few centuries, see Steve McKinion, "Baptism in the Patristic Writings," in *Believer's Baptism: Sign of the New Covenant in Christ* (Nashville: B&H, 2006), 163–88.

practice in that time, know nothing of infant baptism. In fact, their statements on baptism all presuppose the baptism of believers. However, Tertullian's statement in *De Baptismo* (written between 200 and 206) attacking the baptism of infants "constitutes the earliest express mention of infant baptism in the history of the church" and shows that infants were being baptized by the time of Tertullian.[6] Later, in the first half of the third century, Origen believed the baptism of infants to be an apostolic practice.[7] At this point it cannot be said today how widespread the practice was. The practice of infant baptism seems to have originated with the rise of an *ex opere operato* understanding of its effects—it was thought that baptism would secure forgiveness of sins for the baptizee without fail. When Christianity became legal and established, pressure followed for extending church membership to the whole community. By the Council of Carthage in 418, anyone who taught against infant baptism was anathematized.[8] In the sixth century the emperor Justinian made infant baptism mandatory throughout the Roman Empire.

Historical Significance of the Recovery of Believer Baptism

While Roman Catholic, Orthodox, and various dissenting groups continued to practice believer's baptism in the case of converts, there was no general recovery of the practice of baptizing *only* believers until the early sixteenth

---

[6] Jewett, *Infant Baptism*, 21.

[7] See Origen's *Homilies on Luke* (XIV), *Homilies on Leviticus* (VIII), *Commentary on Romans* (V). Cyprian also in his letters advocated the baptism of infants at the earliest age possible (see "Epistle LVIII" in *Ante-Nicene Fathers*, vol. 5, ed. Alexander Roberts and James Donaldson [1886], 353–54). His action was confirmed by a council of 66 pastors at Carthage in 253.

[8] Though even here, David Wright suggested that infant baptism may not have become the norm in practice until the sixth century (D. F. Wright, "At What Ages were People Baptized in the Early Centuries?" *Studia Patristica*, vol. XXX, ed. E. A. Livingstone [Leuven: Peeters, 1997], 389–94). For a review of the evidence concerning the earliest date of infant baptism, see Jewett, *Infant Baptism*, 13–43. Cf. Peter Leithart, "Infant Baptism in History: An Unfinished Tragicomedy," in Strawbridge, ed., *Covenantal Infant Baptism*, 246–61; David Wright, *Infant Baptism in Historical Perspective* (Carlisle, UK: Paternoster, 2007). For a fascinating summary of the archaeological remains of baptismal practices in the early church, see F. M. Buhler, *Baptism*, trans. W. P. Bauman (Dundas, Ontario, Canada: Joshua Press, 2004).

century, when some people, particularly the evangelical
Anabaptists, began to reject the validity of infant baptism.[9]
It is no accident that the nature of true conversion began to
be clarified at the same time the gospel of justification by
faith alone began its recovery. Before the Reformation, most
Christians called themselves Christians largely to affirm the
family, the parish, the town, and even the nation to which
they belonged. The Reformation led to a reappreciation of
the radical nature of Christian conversion. Conversion did
not result from a rite of infancy or from membership within
a particular political entity. It resulted from a self-conscious
profession of faith in God's justifying work in Christ.

The reaffirmation of the authority of Scripture and the
clarity of the gospel led to a surprisingly wide rejection of
the bishop of Rome's authority. As the gospel of justification
by faith alone spread, the impossibility of justification without faith quietly challenged the practice of indiscriminately
administering baptism and the Lord's Supper to everyone
who belonged to a particular political entity, whether city,
nation, or parish. Naturally, this meant that the ancient
Constantinian relationship between church and state was
itself being challenged. Yet only the Anabaptists and the
Baptists were at first willing to rethink ecclesiology and so
reconceive the relationship between church and state, as
examined further below.

In Christian Europe, to reconsider what it meant to
be a Christian required a reconsideration of what it meant
to be a citizen of a city or a nation. Previously, a Christian
could probably imagine other Christians living outside of
one's own nation. Now, by virtue of a Baptist ecclesiology,
it became possible to imagine citizens in one's own nation
who were not Christians or at least were not members of
the same church. From the beginning, ecclesiology has set
Baptists apart from other evangelicals. The doctrine of a visible church composed of only the baptized regenerate is the
hallmark of Baptists.

---

[9] See William Estep, *The Anabaptist Story* (Nashville: Broadman, 1963).

Implications of Gathered Church for Relations with the State

Recapturing the New Testament picture of a church of believers challenged the assumptions most Christians had made since Constantine, namely, that the state is responsible to provide for the church, and the church is responsible for guiding the state. The strongest connection of this sort between church and state continued among Constantine's heirs and others in the Eastern Orthodox areas. In the East what has been called *caesaro-papism* treated the church as the responsibility of the ruler; in effect, to see Caesar as the pope, thus the name. In the West a less centralized and more varied relationship has existed between church and state. Whereas the state typically held the dominant position in the East, especially since the rise of Islam, the church typically had predominance in the West, given its more centralized organization and tradition of enforcing episcopal jurisdiction over rulers. At times emperors were excommunicated, and entire cities were interdicted—unthinkable in the East.

During the Protestant Reformation the leading theologians continued to affirm the traditional Western understanding of the relationship between church and state. Whether a somewhat more passive (Lutheran) or aggressive (Calvinist) stance was taken toward the magistrate's authority, the various reformations effected little immediate change in the church-state relationship. A nation facing a reformation would focus on the questions of which church to recognize and what structure to adopt, two questions about theology and leadership that did not disrupt the basic unit of the European parish. Protestant nations varied in their answers to these questions. But in no magisterial reformation was the local parish dissolved or replaced.[10]

As we have seen, the Baptist denial of infant baptism crucially imperiled the Constantinian church-state settlement

---

[10] The magisterial reformations were those reformations in which the politically established churches were reformed by the political authorities (e.g., the Lutheran, the Anglican, the Calvinist). They get their names from the Latin word *magister*, meaning "master" or "official." Therefore the other reformers (chiefly the Anabaptists) were referred to as the nonmagisterial reformers, meaning that they did not have the backing or support of the government.

in Western Europe.[11] The Baptist belief in regenerate church membership made the relationship between citizens and their church, and thus between church and state, voluntary. This would have been unimaginable in the early and mid-sixteenth century. Ultimately, the Baptist ecclesiology provided the seed for the birth of modern notions of freedom of religion, in which no one church is established and the rights of citizens of every religion are secured. As Christians tried to answer the simple question, "Who should be baptized?" they found that their answer to that question had tremendous effects. If they concluded that only believers should be baptized, that would preclude having a membership that was coextensive with the general population and so effectively would preclude having an established church.

In What Sense Baptism Is a Means of Grace

The Roman Catholic Church teaches that baptism conveys God's grace in and of itself, remitting all sin, both original and actual. The Lutheran Reformation taught that baptism was as certainly effective.[12] Luther in his catechism said, "Baptism works forgiveness of sins, delivers from death and the devil, and gives eternal salvation to all who believe this, as the words and promises of God declare."[13] Calvin, echoing Augustine, called baptism "the visible Word."[14] The Council of Trent (1545–63) anathematized anyone who taught that baptism conferred grace only to those who had faith. The Presbyterian and Reformed understanding has treated baptism as a sign and seal of God's grace.[15]

---

[11] This was so much the case that Anabaptists and Baptists throughout the sixteenth and seventeenth centuries repeatedly needed to publicly disavow anarchism.

[12] When pressed in conversation about historical Lutheran statements affirming the necessity and saving power of baptism and how those statements can be squared with justification by faith alone, some Lutheran theologians recently told this author that one may be saved without baptism but one may not be saved without faith.

[13] See John Theodore Mueller, *Christian Dogmatics* (St. Louis: Concordia, 1955), 494–95.

[14] See Calvin, *Institutes*, IV.xiv.6.

[15] The Belgic Confession (article 33) says that baptism and the Lord's Supper "are visible signs and seals of an invisible thing, by means whereof God works in us by the power of the Holy Spirit." Cf. Charles Hodge, *Systematic Theology*, vol. 3 (1871; repr. Grand Rapids: Eerdmans, 1952), 582.

Among Baptists, baptism has never been treated as an essential conduit for God's grace. Rather, they have regarded it as a command given to new believers and therefore the normal means for marking and celebrating their salvation. Baptism is a visible sermon, informed by the Word, and entirely dependent on God's Spirit to create the spiritual reality it depicts. In the baptism of a believer, "there is the blessing of God's favor that comes with all obedience, as well as the joy that comes through public profession of one's faith, and the reassurance of having a clear physical picture of dying and rising with Christ and of washing away sins."[16]

The Lord's Supper

Baptism has not been the only ordinance beset by controversy in the history of the church. The Lord's Supper in its nature and effects has been variously construed. These various interpretations have helped distinguish Roman Catholic theology from Protestant and have also led to differences between Protestants. At its center the discussion has settled on the question, "What is the relation of Christ to his Supper?"

Transubstantiation

Fully developed by Thomas Aquinas and confirmed at the Fourth Lateran Council (1215), the doctrine of transubstantiation describes the Lord's Supper as a re-presentation of the sacrifice of Christ. Aquinas argued the substance of the bread in the celebration of the Eucharist changes into Christ's physical body, while the substance of the wine changes into his physical blood.[17] Why then do the bread and wine not change in appearance? Aquinas's response depended on a philosophical distinction, drawn from Aristotle, between the accident, or the outward form, and substance, or inner essence, of a thing. Only the substance of the bread and wine change, said Aquinas, thus the word "transubstantiation." The accidents, or those characteristics

---

[16] Wayne Grudem, *Systematic Theology* (Grand Rapids: Zondervan, 1994), 980–81.
[17] Aquinas, *Summa Theologica,* part 3, questions 75–77.

which impress themselves upon human senses, remain unchanged.

The Eucharist is understood to be a real and effective "unbloody sacrifice." All who partake of it, aside from those who have committed a mortal sin, receive God's grace. Merely witnessing a mass counts as a participatory act worthy of that grace. More often communicants receive the consecrated wafer which is understood to be the transubstantiated body of Christ. Since Vatican II (1962–65) laypersons have more often been allowed to participate in the cup. Proponents of transubstantiation often apply Christ's promises in John 6:53–57 to the Lord's Supper, even though he had not yet established the Supper.[18]

Consubstantiation

Consubstantiation denies the literal and essential transformation of the bread and wine into Christ's essence, but it proposes the body and blood of Christ join together with ("con" being the Latin prefix for "with") the substance of the bread and wine at the Lord's table. Lutheran theologians have described the body and blood of Christ as "in, with and under" the physical bread and wine.[19] As Luther's Small Catechism teaches, "What is the Sacrament of the Altar? It is the true body and blood of our Lord Jesus Christ, under the bread and wine, for us Christian to eat and to drink, instituted by Christ himself."[20] Luther's view allowed him to continue holding a deep reverence toward the elements (and one should never underestimate the effect of popular piety on theology), while also ridding himself of a logical problem of Rome's view, namely, that something appears to be what it is not (its accidents and substance no longer agree). This doctrine of consubstantiation continues to be the teaching of Lutheran theologians.[21]

---

[18] Joseph Pohle, *The Sacraments: A Dogmatic Treatise*, vol. 2, ed. Arthur Preuss (St. Louis: B. Herder, 1942), 25.
[19] See Mueller, *Christian Dogmatics*, 510.
[20] Cf. Augsburg Confession, article X.
[21] E.g., Mueller, *Christian Dogmatics*, 509–20.

Spiritual Presence

John Calvin taught that Christ really is present in his Supper, but his presence is not physical, as the Roman Catholics and Lutherans taught, but spiritual.[22] This spiritual presence is perceived and profited from by faith, not by the physical senses. Apart from faith the Supper is not effective. According to this understanding, "in exchange for a personal claim on and actual possession of all this wealth [in Christ], believers express faith in Christ as Savior and pledge obedience to him as Lord and King."[23] As the Westminster Confession puts it, Christ's body and blood are "really, but spiritually, present to the faith of believers." They "really and indeed, yet not carnally and corporally but spiritually, receive, and feed upon, Christ crucified, and all the benefits of his death."[24]

Memorial

Of the four views of the Lord's Supper detailed here, only the Supper as memorial is universally accepted. Advocates for the other three positions go beyond the Supper as memorial, but no one denies this is an aspect of the Lord's Supper. Paul was unambiguous: "Whenever you eat this bread and drink this cup, you proclaim the Lord's death until he comes" (1 Cor 11:26). So it is not surprising that memorialist language is found frequently in the history of the church, from Clement of Alexandria to Origen, from Cyril of Jerusalem to John Chrysostom. Even Augustine frequently used such language. This view came to prominence in the Reformation along with a denial of the physical presence of Christ in the Supper.

Huldrych Zwingli taught that the Lord's Supper is a re-presentation of Christ's sacrifice but only in the symbolic sense of proclaiming it again.[25] Zwingli pointed to Paul's

---

[22] Calvin, *Institutes*, IV.xvii.9–12. Cf. Berkhof, *Systematic Theology*, 653–54. Calvin received serious criticism on this point from later Reformed theologians like William Cunningham, Charles Hodge, and Robert Lewis Dabney.

[23] Erickson, *Christian Theology*, 1127.

[24] Westminster Confession, XXIX.vii.

[25] Cf. Strong, *Systematic Theology*, 538–43. Charles Hodge saw little difference between Zwingli and Calvin on this point (Hodge, *Systematic Theology*, vol. 3, 626–31). The present author agrees with Hodge.

words in 1 Cor 11:24–26 as the clearest biblical testimony
for how the Supper should be understood. Since Zwingli,
many Protestants, including most Baptists, have adopted this
memorial understanding, primarily because it is indubitably
biblical, and secondarily (perhaps) because it avoids any hint
of the sacramentalism of the Roman Catholic position. That
said, Baptists have historically used language so rich about
Christ's presence in the Lord's Supper for those who come by
faith that little difference is perceptible between their position and the Reformed idea of Christ's spiritual presence.[26]

In What Sense Is the Supper a Means of Grace?

The chief division about the way in which the Lord's
Supper is a means of grace in the lives of Christians is
the same division that is found in understanding baptism.
The basic dividing question is, What is the relation of faith
to the ordinance? Does the participant's faith make the ordinance a means of God's grace, or does the ordinance bestow
grace regardless of faith? Among Baptists, the Lord's Supper
has not been regarded as an essential conduit for God's
grace. Rather, it has been regarded as a command given to
new believers, and therefore the normal means of marking
out those who have been separated from the world and given
fellowship with Christ. Like baptism, the Lord's Supper presents a visible sermon, and it is entirely dependent on God's
Spirit to create the spiritual communion between God and
believers that it depicts.

C. H. Spurgeon's mid-nineteenth-century catechism
well represents this view. In answer to Question 80, "What is
the Lord's Supper?" Spurgeon wrote:

---

[26] In fact, Wayne Grudem represents these two views together as the view of "The
Rest of Protestantism," in his *Systematic Theology*, 995–96. Cf. Ligon Duncan,
"True Communion with Christ: Calvin, Westminster and Consensus on the Lord's
Supper," in *The Westminster Confession into the 21st Century*, vol. 2 (Rosshire,
Scotland: Christian Focus, 2003), 429–75; W. G. T. Shedd, *Dogmatic Theology*
3rd ed., ed. Alan W. Gomes (Phillipsburg: P&R, 2003), 814. Cf. Lutheran theo-
logian Mueller, *Christian Dogmatics*, 509. "Calvin's doctrine was nothing but a
polished form of Zwingli's crude teaching, couched in phrases approaching the
Lutheran terminology as closely as possible" (F. Bente, cited in Mueller, *Christian
Dogmatics*, 514).

> The Lord's Supper is an ordinance of the New Testament, instituted by Jesus Christ; wherein, by giving and receiving bread and wine, according to his appointment, his death is shown forth, (1 Cor 11:23–26) and the worthy receivers are, not after a corporeal and carnal manner, but by faith, made partakers of his body and blood, with all his benefits, to their spiritual nourishment, and growth in grace.[27]

Communion: Closed, Close, or Open?

Baptists have disagreed about what faithfulness to Paul's exhortation in 1 Cor 11:27–31 implies. Indeed, there has been a wide spectrum among Baptist Christians about who are proper participants in the Lord's Supper.[28] These can be generally summarized in three positions (though there are almost an infinite number of variations). The first position is called "strict," or "closed," communion. Many Baptists, particularly in the seventeenth and eighteenth centuries and among Landmarkists in the nineteenth and twentieth centuries, have taught that only members of the local congregation celebrating the Lord's Supper should be allowed

---

[27] Spurgeon echoed emphases of the Second London Confession (1689; chap. 30, paragraph 7): "Worthy receivers, outwardly partaking of the visible Elements in this Ordinance, do then also inwardly by faith, really and indeed, yet not carnally, and corporally, but spiritually receive, and feed upon Christ crucified & all the benefits of his death: the Body and Blood of Christ, being then not corporally, or carnally, but spiritually present to the faith of Believers, in that Ordinance, as the Elements themselves are to their outward senses." In this the Baptist ministers adopted the language entirely of the Westminster Confession (from 1646; chap. 29, paragraph 7) except for changing the word "sacrament" to "ordinance," and omitting the description of how the body of Christ is not corporally present "in, with, or under the bread and wine."

[28] See Peter Naylor, *Calvinism, Communion and the Baptists: A Study of English Calvinistic Baptists from the Late 1600s to the Early 1800s*, in *Studies in Baptist History and Thought* (Carlisle, UK: Paternoster, 2003). The classic defense of the Southern Baptist position was penned in 1846 by R. B. C. Howell, at the time the pastor of Second Baptist Church, Richmond, Virginia, and later the pastor of First Baptist Church, Nashville, Tennessee. Howell articulated a non-Landmarkist position of close communion that is still instructive for Baptists today, wondering why they should exclude from membership or participation of the Lord's Supper paedo-Baptists. See Howell's *The Terms of Communion at the Lord's Table* (Philadelphia: American Baptist Publication Society, 1846). There is a vast literature of nineteenth-century Baptist works on proper terms for admission to the Lord's table which would be a fruitful field of study for Christians today wanting to better understand church membership.

to partake of the Supper when celebrated by its church. "Close" communion has usually referred to a position advocated throughout Baptist history—but advocated more widely in the late eighteenth and early nineteenth centuries in the wake of the evangelical revivals—that would say that all of those believers who have been baptized as believers are welcomed to the Lord's table.[29] "Open" communion, again a position advocated throughout Baptist history (for example by John Bunyan) but becoming dominant only in the twentieth century, advocates that all who know themselves to be trusting in Christ for salvation, regardless of whether they had been baptized as believers, are welcomed to the Lord's table.

---

[29] Added to this requirement of having been baptized is naturally the requirement that the self-professed believer also be a regular member of another evangelical congregation where they are also allowed to take the Lord's Supper. This kind of occasional communion would allow for what has been called "occasional communion," respecting the membership and discipline of other congregations.

11

The History of the
Organization of the Church

Other than the role of the ordinances, the main ecclesiological disputes throughout the history of Christianity have occurred over matters of the church's organization. In particular three areas have drawn much of the disagreement: membership, government, and discipline. The third area is so intertwined with the first two that in times past a written work that dealt with all three topics might simply be called a "discipline." Someone must determine who is in and who is out of earthly communities (if corrective discipline is to be practiced); and that necessarily involves coming to conclusions about who has that right and responsibility, what processes determine inclusion in and exclusion from the community, and what the requirements of being "in" are.

Membership

Baptist Practice

Given that the New Testament restricts baptism to believers, Baptists have concluded that church membership is restricted to individuals who have made a credible profession of faith. The profession of faith should include submitting to believer's baptism and making oneself accountable to a particular local congregation with whom the professing believer regularly communes. These conclusions led both European Anabaptists in the early sixteenth century and various English separatists in the sixteenth and seventeenth centuries to separate themselves from the established churches. They instead espoused a "gathered" congregation, which was a revolutionary idea. Not everyone born in a certain geographic area, they said, should be baptized and confirmed in church membership. Rather, congregations should be composed of the faithful who gather together voluntarily upon their own profession of faith, desiring to unite with others in the same area and form a Christian congregation.

Covenants and Their Use

In connection with these new voluntary gatherings, church covenants began to be used. Christians had certainly made pledges to one another before the sixteenth century, but the situation brought about by the Protestant Reformation created a fresh need for such pledges.[1] If the boundaries of a parish could no longer define who should be included in a congregation's membership, what could? For many Christians the answer became subscription to a church covenant. Charles Deweese defined a church covenant as "a series of written pledges based on the Bible which church members voluntarily make to God and to one another regarding their basic moral and spiritual commitments and the practice of their faith."[2] Sixteenth-century Protestants, particularly the continental Anabaptists, the Scottish Reformers, and the English separatists and Congregationalists, began using church covenants. Even

---

[1] Writing in AD 112, Pliny referred to Christians making certain moral pledges to one another. Such covenants were also practiced by the followers of Jan Hus. See Charles W. Deweese, *Baptist Church Covenants* (Nashville: Broadman, 1990), 19–23.

[2] Deweese, *Baptist Church Covenants*, viii.

the 1527 Schleitheim Confession of the Anabaptists contains an element of covenanting.[3]

By the seventeenth century, church covenants continued in use not only among Independent congregations in
England and America but also among Baptists who adopted
their usage, especially Particular Baptists. From the seventeenth to the nineteenth centuries, church covenants, often
accompanied by a statement of faith, acted as the most basic
document of a Baptist congregation. As recently as the late
nineteenth century, Baptist congregations commonly gathered several days before celebrating communion in order to
prepare for the Lord's Supper by reaffirming their covenant
together. Over the last century, however, church covenants
have had little role in the life of most Baptist congregations.
Expectations of members (whether expressed in covenants,
or by the practice of church discipline) seem out of character in an age in which congregations vie with one another
for members.[4]

Confessions and Their Use

If a church covenant represents the agenda (things to be
done) of a local congregation, statements of faith or confessions represent their credenda (things to be believed). From
the earliest times Christians have practiced summarizing
the content of their faith. Peter made the first Christian declaration of faith when he said, "You are the Christ" (Mark
8:29). Paul wrote to the Corinthian Christians,

> What I received I passed on to you as of first impor-
> tance: that Christ died for our sins according to the
> Scriptures, that he was buried, that he was raised on
> the third day according to the Scriptures, and that
> he appeared to Peter, and then to the Twelve. (1 Cor
> 15:3–5)

---

[3] See Daniel L. Akin, "An Expositional Analysis of the Schleitheim Confession,"
CTR 2, no. 2 (Spring 1988): 345–70.
[4] Deweese suggested a number of factors which have led to the decline in the use
of the church covenant among Baptists in America (*Baptist Church Covenants*,
88–91).

In the early church simple formularies like the Apostles' Creed were developed for dealing with baptismal candidates. And Christians were shepherded away from heretical teachings with more complex and careful statements like the Christological definitions of the Nicene Creed (AD 325/381) and the Definition of Faith at Chalcedon (451).

The Protestant Reformation spawned numerous confessions: the Augsburg Confession (Lutheran), the Thirty-nine Articles (Church of England), the Belgic Confession (Reformed), the Westminster Confession of Faith (Presbyterian), and many more. Baptists also produced confessions of faith. In fact, Baptists produced more than any other group because of their decentralized, congregational polity. In 1611, for example, Thomas Helwys, one of the first Baptists in England, led a number of Christians to write a confession of faith. From the seventeenth century on, it has been common for Baptists to summarize the content of their faith in a confession, both for making their beliefs clear to outsiders and for having an explicit common ground of unity for the members of their own congregation.[5] Confessions of faith have played a vital role in the history of Baptist congregations.[6] As J. L. Reynolds concluded, "The use of a confession of faith, so far from disparaging the authority of the Bible, as a standard, really exalts it."[7]

Polity: Forms of Government

A second aspect of the church's life that has developed over its history has been its polity or organization. Every group must determine how it will be governed. Churches, likewise, must have procedures for determining who is a member and who is not and who is the final earthly judicatory under God to give leadership, settle controversies, and

[5] Standard collections of Baptist confessions of faith have been assembled by W. J. McGlothlin, *Baptist Confessions of Faith* (Philadelphia: American Baptist Publication Society, 1911); and William L. Lumpkin, *Baptist Confessions of Faith* (Valley Forge, PA: Judson Press, 1959). For a defense of the use of confessions among Baptists, see Reynolds, *Church Polity*, 334–42.
[6] E.g., the Second London Confession (1689), the New Hampshire Confession (1833), and the Baptist Faith and Message (1925, 1963, 2000).
[7] Reynolds, *Church Polity*, 340.

so forth. To these questions several different answers have been given.

Bishops

One of the earliest answers to the question of who should govern was "the bishop." As demonstrated earlier, the word "bishop" (*episkopos*) in the New Testament is used interchangeably with the words for elder and pastor. The sayings in the New Testament which underscore the authority of church leaders (e.g., Heb 13:7,17; 1 Pet 5:2) point to the pastor as the one who possesses responsibility and authority in the church. By the second century the pastors of leading cities and towns had accrued increased authority, sometimes including over churches in nearby, newly evangelized areas.[8] From the second through the fourth centuries, the diocese (taken from the Latin word for a district in Roman civil administration) developed as an ecclesiastical area with a single bishop as its head. Though their duties and responsibilities vary, bishops in this sense are recognized by most churches, including the Eastern Orthodox churches, the Roman Catholic Church, Lutheran churches, Anglican churches, and Methodist churches. The Eastern Orthodox and Roman Catholic churches regard this office as divinely established.

The Lutheran, Anglican, and Methodist churches, on the other hand, simply recognize the office as useful and expedient. In the last two centuries, many Episcopalian churches have democratized their structures, even submitting bishops to decisions made by representative bodies of clergy and laity. At the same time collections of congregations in many Pentecostal and charismatic circles began to recognize extracongregational authority for some bishops. Whole "apostolic networks" have grown up around the ministries of particular individuals.

The Pope

The Roman Catholic Church is distinguished from other Christian communions by its submission to and dependence

---

[8] A good example of this would be the authority that Ignatius had as a bishop. He advocated that this authority legitimately belonged to the bishop.

on the bishop of Rome, the pope. While pope (*papas*) was a common way to address certain bishops in the early church, it was increasingly restricted to the bishop of Rome between the sixth and the eighth centuries, particularly in the West. Rome, the former capital of the Roman Empire, was regarded as the central and principal bishopric. The Eastern and Western churches broke communion in 1054 over the Western church's (and especially Gregory VII's) insistence that the bishop of Rome be recognized as the supreme head of the universal church. The West maintained (and maintains) that Christ declared Peter the first among equals and the chief of the apostles upon Peter's confession (Matt 16:16–19). Peter then became the first bishop of Rome, and those who succeed him inherit his authority as well. Thus the Roman Catholic Church recognizes the pope as the vicar of Christ, the head of the church on earth, with the authority to ratify and so define tradition.

Presbyterianism

With the advent of the Protestant Reformation, fresh interest was shown in the Bible's teaching on the structure of the church. The New Testament evidence for the plurality of elders (cited above) was rediscovered. And groups of ministers (called consistories) were put forward as appropriate replacements for bishops in the Swiss cantons that were reforming in the early- and mid-sixteenth century. Following the work of Heinrich Bullinger in Zurich and John Calvin in Geneva, others began to organize according to a Presbyterian system. Reformed congregations sprung up in the Netherlands, Scotland, Hungary, Germany, Poland, and France. In Scotland, John Knox took on the challenge of reforming the established church of an entire nation along the lines of this system he felt to be biblical. The nationwide General Assembly became the final arbiter recognized in the Church of Scotland. Thomas Cartwright at Cambridge began teaching presbyterianism in 1570 in his lectures on the book of Acts.

Though presbyterianism was a strong force for reforming the established church in England throughout the seventeenth century, it never became the polity of the Church of England. Presbyterian structures came to North America with the European settlers from Scotland and the Netherlands, where they have flourished. They have also flourished around the world, from Korea to Africa. Most Presbyterian bodies are connectional. In the United States the (national) general assembly of any Presbyterian body usually functions as the final arbiter in ecclesiastical matters, with regional synods and/or presbyteries ruling beneath them and with sessions (boards of elders) of a local congregation below them.[9] Some independent churches are presbyterian in the sense that they are ruled by a board of elders, but they have no court of appeal outside of that congregation's own elders. Presbyterians generally teach that the principles of their organization, not the particulars, are taught in Scripture.[10]

Congregationalism's Development

At the time of the Reformation, churches, which were gathered not by a ruler or magistrate but by the shared convictions of individual Christians, began to organize, recognizing themselves as their own final earthly authority in religious matters.

Early in the Reformation, Martin Luther strongly advocated recognizing the congregation's responsibility to determine who would preach God's Word to them regularly. Reasoning from a wide variety of Scriptures—such as John 10:4–8 about the sheep's knowledge; warning the sheep about false teachers, as if they could do something about them in Matt 7:15; and the pattern of electing deacons in Acts 6:1–6—Luther concluded that, as he entitled one tract in 1523, *A Christian Assembly or Congregation Has the Right and Power to Judge All Teaching and to Call,*

---

[9] A fine, concise explanation of Presbyterian government is Sean Michael Lucas, *What Is Church Government?* (Phillipsburg, NJ: P&R, 2009).

[10] For an exception to their general posture, see Robert Reymond, "The Presbytery-Led Church: Presbyterian Church Government," in Chad Brand and R. Stanton Norman, eds., *Perspectives on Church Government: Five Views of Church Polity* (Nashville: B&H, 2004), 87–138.

Appoint, and Dismiss Teachers, Established and Proven by Scripture.[11]

In England advocates of a congregational polity arose in the 1580s. Robert Browne's *A Treatise of Reformation Without Tarrying for Any* (1582) and Henry Barrow's *A True Description out of the Word of God of the Visible Church* (1589) laid out a doctrine of polity which was not reliant on structures above the local congregation. In the 1630s, as many Christians began to regard the structures of the Church of England as incorrigible, congregationalism found new and prominent advocates.

John Cotton, John Owen, and Thomas Goodwin advocated "the congregational way." In 1658, the Savoy Declaration (an adaptation of the Westminster Confession) laid out congregational principles of church government.[12] By the time of

---

[11] *Luther's Works*, vol. 39, trans. Eric W. and Ruth C. Gritsch (Philadelphia: Fortress, 1970), 301–14.

[12] In the section on "The Institution of Churches" appended to the Declaration of Faith, the Savoy divines declared: "IV. To each of these Churches thus gathered, according unto his minde declared in his Word, he hath given all that Power and Authority, which is any way needful for their carrying on that Order in Worship and Discipline, which he hath instituted for them to observe with Commands and Rules, for the due and right exerting and executing of that Power. V. These particular Churches thus appointed by the Authority of Christ, and intrusted with power from him for the ends before expressed, are each of them as unto those ends, the seat of that Power which he is pleased to communicate to his Saints of Subjects in this world, so that as such they receive it immediately from himself. VI. Besides these particular Churches, there is not instituted by Christ any Church more extensive or Catholique entrusted with power for the administration of his Ordinances, or the execution of any authority in his name" (A. G. Matthews, ed., *The Savoy Declaration of Faith and Order 1658* [London: Independent Press, 1959], 121–22). Would such an understanding contradict those "more extensive" organizations—like central authority in a multisite church—in the same way it intended to contradict Episcopalian and Presbyterian claims to exercise the authority of Christ outside of and over local congregations? For a careful, detailed study of debates around this time about the keys of authority that Christ committed to his church, see Hunter Powell, "The Dissenting Brethren and the Power of the Keys, 1640–1644" (Unpublished Ph.D. dissertation; Cambridge University, 2011). Powell concluded that the most significant seventeenth-century defense of congregationalism was John Cotton's 1644 work, *The Keys of the Kingdom of Heaven*. (For a modern edition of Cotton's *Keys*, see Larzer Ziff, ed., *John Cotton on the Churches of New England* [Cambridge: Harvard University Press, 1968] 71–164). For a modern distillation and analysis of Cotton's *Keys*, see Powell, "Dissenting Brethren," chaps. 4–5. For a Congregationalist critique of Samuel Rutherford's Scottish Presbyterian polity, see Thomas Hooker, *A Survey of the Summe of Church-Discipline* (1648). Perhaps the most comprehensive explanation and defense of congregationalism of this period is Thomas Goodwin, *The Right Order and Government of the Churches of Christ* (1696).

the American Revolution, two out of every five Christians in the American colonies were in some kind of congregational church, whether Congregationalist or Baptist. Today many independent churches are congregational in structure. Baptist churches are also congregational. Such congregational churches have often joined together voluntarily in local associations and national unions or conventions.

The Rights and Responsibilities of Congregations

Advocates of congregationalism understand that the Bible teaches the local congregation is ultimately responsible for its discipline and doctrine. Disputes between members (Matt 18:15–17), as well as matters of doctrine (Gal 1:8; 2 Tim 4:3), church discipline (1 Corinthians 5), and membership (2 Cor 2:6–8) are all recognized as congregational matters. No other authority may obtrude itself into the position of giving final correction to the congregation or overruling them on such matters. Nor may the congregation delegate this authority to an elder or bishop or any other structure, thereby deferring their own accountability before God for doctrine or discipline.

Church Discipline

Historical data on the life of the church immediately after the New Testament period is only intermittent and partial. The church was, after all, a small and sometimes illegal group. Written sources multiply greatly after the Christian church was legalized throughout the empire under Constantine. For the 1200 years between Constantine and the Protestant Reformation, church discipline, whether by individual excommunication or interdict (withholding the sacraments from the population of a political entity), was often used more to protect the church's corporate interests against the claims of the state than to reclaim Christians from sin and protect the gospel's witness.

When the leaders of the Reformation began to recover a more biblical understanding of preaching and administrating the sacraments as the two marks of a true church,

the recovery of church discipline as a consequent mark followed. Implied in the right administration of the sacraments
was the correct practice of church discipline. After all, if
marking out the church from the world is one function of
the sacraments, then discipline becomes the mechanism for
enforcing that mandate. The right discipline of the church
became so significant that it began to be presented as a third
mark of a true church.[13]

The twenty-ninth article of the Belgic Confession (1561)
stated:

> The marks by which the true Church is known are
> these: If the pure doctrine of the gospel is preached
> therein; if she maintains the pure administration of
> the sacraments as instituted by Christ; if church dis-
> cipline is exercised in punishing of sin; in short, if all
> things are managed according to the pure Word of
> God, all things contrary thereto rejected, and Jesus
> Christ acknowledged as the only Head of the Church.[14]

In our own day Edmund Clowney has summarized these
marks as "true preaching of the Word; proper observance of
the sacraments; and faithful exercise of church discipline."[15]

While some Anabaptist groups like the Mennonites practiced banning, or social exclusion, this was exceptional. The
most well-known example of church discipline in American
history—the scarlet "A" sewed on Hester Prynne's clothes—
was a product of novelist Nathaniel Hawthorne's historical
imagination and not an accurate record of either a historical event or of the general practice of church discipline in
colonial New England. In the vast majority of cases, whether
in Presbyterian, Congregational, Baptist, or Methodist

---

[13] For an example of a modern popular treatment, see D. Martyn Lloyd-Jones, *The Church and the Last Things*, vol. 3, *Great Doctrines of the Bible* (Wheaton, IL: Crossway, 1998), 13–18.
[14] Cf. the Scotch Confession (1560), Article 18: "The trew preaching of the Worde of God . . . the right administration of the sacraments of Christ Jesus . . . Ecclesiastical discipline uprightlie ministered."
[15] Clowney, *Church*, 101. In this book Clowney has a good summary of the marks of the church considered biblically, historically, and in context of current questions of church versus parachurch (see pp. 99–115).

churches, congregational exclusion meant barring the sinner from communion and, ultimately, membership until repentance occurred.

Baptists, being committed to regenerate membership in the visible church, were vigorous practitioners of church discipline. Greg Wills's research shows that in Georgia, pre-Civil War "southern Baptists excommunicated nearly 2 percent of their membership every year," and yet at the same time the membership in Baptist churches grew at twice the rate of the general population.[16] Though fruitful and beneficial to the gospel, the work of confronting and disciplining was never easy. Basil Manly Jr. expressed his own "profound grief" over one case of discipline in the church he pastored.[17]

So why did this practice end? Wills convincingly argued that discipline among Baptists

> declined partly because it became more burdensome in larger churches. Young Baptists refused in increasing numbers to submit to discipline for dancing, and the churches shrank from excluding them. Urban churches, pressed by the need for large buildings and the desire for refined music and preaching, subordinated church discipline to the task of keeping the church solvent. . . . They lost the resolve to purge their churches of straying members. No one publicly advocated the demise of discipline. No Baptist leader arose to call for an end to congregational censures. No theologians argued that discipline was unsound in principle or practice. . . . It simply faded away, as if Baptists had grown weary of holding one another accountable.[18]

---

[16] Greg Wills, *Democratic Religion: Freedom, Authority and Church Discipline in the Baptist South 1785–1900* (New York: Oxford University Press, 1997), 22.
[17] Ibid., 119.
[18] Ibid., 9. Cf. "Church discipline presupposed a stark dichotomy between the norms of society and the kingdom of God. The more evangelicals purified the society, the less they felt the urgency of a discipline that separated the church from the world" (Wills, *Democratic Religion*, 10). "Activism became the crowning virtue of Baptist piety in the twentieth century" (Wills, *Democratic Religion*, 133). On documenting the decline, see Stephen Haines, "Southern Baptist Church Discipline, 1880–1939," *Baptist History and Heritage*, vol. XX, no. 2 (April 1985): 14–27.

And what was the result? John Dagg put it provocatively: "When discipline leaves a church, Christ goes with it."[19]

By the twentieth century the absence of church discipline was generally assumed and only occasionally observed as a problem.[20] In 1944 Greek scholar H. E. Dana observed:

> The abuse of discipline is reprehensible and destructive, but not more than the abandonment of discipline. Two generations ago the churches were applying discipline in a vindictive and arbitrary fashion which justly brought it into disrepute; today the pendulum has swung to the other extreme—discipline is almost wholly neglected. It is time for a new generation of pastors to restore this important function of the church to its rightful significance and place in church life.[21]

It is questionable whether the generation of pastors in the 1940s heeded Dana's call. However, as the surrounding culture has become more overtly immoral, twenty-first-century churches show some signs of recovering practices that promote the purity of the church, including the practice of corrective church discipline.

Through all the changes of the centuries, Christians can be confident that the survival of the church is not ultimately based on human faithfulness. In both the parable of the growing seed, in which Christ taught that, whether the sower sleeps or gets up, "the seed sprouts and grows" (Mark 4:27), and in Christ's promise that "the gates of Hades will not overcome [the church]" (Matt 16:18), Christ has given a sure pledge of his church's success. In everything from the church's obedience to its life and organization, the span of church history is a demonstration of Christ's faithfulness to his promises.

---

[19] John L. Dagg, *A Treatise on Church Order* (Charleston, SC: Southern Baptist Publication Society, 1858), 274.
[20] E.g., Josef Nordenhaug, "Baptists and Regenerate Church Membership," *R&E*, vol. LX, no. 2 (Spring 1963): 135–48; and James Leo Garrett Jr., *Baptist Church Discipline* (Nashville: Broadman, 1962).
[21] H. E. Dana, *Manual of Ecclesiology* (Kansas City, KS: Central Seminary Press, 1944), 244.

Part 3

How Does It All Fit Together?

12

A Protestant Church: Putting Together the Marks of the Church

I n order to be faithful to what the Bible teaches about the church's nature, shape, and outline, we must consider both what Christians have said in the past and what systematic conclusions have been established over the course of the church's history. And we do this always in the context of holding these findings up to the light of our own study of Scripture. Ultimately, we find that the various challenges which confronted the church through history have led to a clearer, more defined set of affirmations and entailments. By affirming the sufficiency of Scripture and the requisite role of faith in participating in the ordinances, we can conclude that a biblically faithful church is a Protestant church. By affirming the necessarily voluntary and consensual nature of membership in a local congregation, we can conclude that a biblically faithful church is a gathered church. By affirming the nature and polity of a local congregation, we can conclude that a biblically faithful church is a congregational church. And by affirming Christ's command to baptize only those who believe and obey, we can conclude that a biblically faithful church is a baptistic church. In this section each of these descriptions is examined in order to see how the Bible's teachings fit together in the life of a local church.

If in fact the Bible teaches that God creates a people for himself through his Word, then preaching takes a central role in the life of the church. And if in fact the Bible teaches that baptism and the Lord's Supper mark off the visible church from the world, then their correct administration is linked to faith in God's promises. Both of these understandings find expression in the biblical teachings of the Protestant Reformers.

The Centrality of Preaching

The center and source of the congregation's life is the Word of God. God's promises to his people in Scripture create and sustain his people. Therefore the congregation is responsible to ensure, as much as lies within its power, that the Word of God is preached at its regular meetings.

By the sixteenth century the centrality of the Word had long been displaced by the sacraments, especially by the sacrament of the Eucharist. In the face of this near universal distortion, the Reformers correctly returned to Scripture to find a canon, or rule, against which to measure the Roman church's current teaching. In 1539, Luther wrote, "God's Word cannot be without God's people, and conversely, God's people cannot be without God's Word."[1] The central role played by the Word in the New Testament church (e.g., 6:42; Acts 20:40–47; 2 Tim 4:2) was recovered in the teachings and lives of the Protestant Reformers. "The church is not a group of people groping for a philosophy of life congenial to modern conditions, but a living body already being shaped by apostolic teaching. Holding steady to that teaching is a principal mark of the authenticity of the church."[2]

---

[1] Martin Luther, "On the Councils and the Church" trans. Charles M. Jacobs, *Luther's Works*, vol. 41 (Philadelphia: Fortress Press, 1966), 150.
[2] Thomas Oden, *Classic Christianity* (New York: HarperOne, 1992), 752. Edmund Clowney said, "God is not only present in the midst of his people. He speaks. The ministry of the Word of God in worship partakes of the solemnity of the occasion. Solemnity does not mean joylessness, for the Word calls to praise. Yet the authority of the Word of the Lord remains central for Christian worship" (Clowney, "The

If the Scriptures are "the word of life" (Phil 2:16), they should both generate and regulate the church's life. Christians gather in congregations to hear one who stands in the place of God by giving his Word to his people. Through preaching, Christians come to know and understand God and his Word. It is a word to which Christians contribute nothing other than hearing and heeding.

A Christian sermon is, even in its method, a picture of God's grace. Since faith comes by hearing (Rom 10:17), hearing God's Word rather than seeing the mass is appropriately placed at the center of the congregation's public assembly. Christians rely on God's Word, so preaching the Word must be absolutely central. And the preaching which most exemplifies this is expositional preaching—preaching in which the point of the passage of Scripture is the point of the message. Scripture is both authoritative and sufficient, and that should be evident in Christian gatherings.

The Visibility of the Church

The Protestant rediscovery of the biblical truth of justification by faith alone was a recovery of the biblical gospel.[3] As Protestant congregations replaced sacramental ritualism with gospel preaching, the sacraments (or ordinances) themselves took on another purpose, or really, their original biblical purposes—marking out the church from the world and providing a visible picture of the gospel message accepted by faith. As a result the church became defined not by individuals who were baptized and who witnessed the mass but by individuals who personally believed the promises set forth in baptism and the Lord's Supper and who therefore participated in those rituals. Even Protestants who practiced infant baptism did not teach baptism effected salvation. They taught that it reflected salvation and that salvation would only come to pass if the one baptized believed, whether

Biblical Theology of the Church," in *The Church in the Bible and the World*, ed. D. A. Carson [Grand Rapids: Baker, 1987], 22).

[3] For a, brief, accurate, and edifying recounting of the Protestant Reformation, including its relation to the doctrine of the church, see Michael Reeves, *The Unquenchable Flame* (Nashville: B&H, 2009).

before or after his or her baptism. Therefore, faith became the essence of what separated the church from the world. This faith was given visible form in the ordinances. Thus the church is, as James Bannerman described it, "an outward and public witness for God on the earth."[4]

Faith's role in distinguishing the visible church from the world makes the Protestant church what it is. Faith shows itself initially in the believer's submission to baptism and then repeatedly in his or her participation in the Lord's Supper. Whereas obedience and submission to the visible church were also emphasized in the Roman Catholic Church, Protestant churches were marked by adherents who expressed personal faith in Christ, apart from which baptism and the Lord's Supper would be useless.

The Protestant impulse to place faith at the center of the ordinances has shown itself in many ways, from the presence of numerous Baptist movements, to American colonial minister Jonathan Edwards's adoption of believers-only communion.

In summary, Christianity requires a conscious belief in the gospel. When God's authoritative Word is taught, it must be consciously believed and trusted. This trust, or faith, is what distinguishes God's people, who have made an initial confession in baptism and a continuing confession through participation in the Lord's Supper. When the sufficiency of Scripture and the necessity of faith in practicing the ordinances are affirmed, it becomes clear that a biblically faithful church is a Protestant church.

---

[4] James Bannerman, *The Church of Christ*, vol. 1 (repr., Edinburgh: Banner of Truth, 1960), 1.

13

A Gathered Church: Putting Together the Membership of the Church

I n addition to being a Protestant church, a biblically faithful church is a gathered church. It is a voluntarily assembled congregation that is not bound together by nationality, ethnicity, or family alone. No mere circumstance of birth should determine the membership of a biblically faithful church. Rather, a profession of faith in Christ and the act of submitting to the teachings and discipline of a particular church should regulate a congregation's membership. Christians choose to gather together regularly out of obedience to God's Word.

For centuries historical circumstances obscured the voluntary nature of the church. The Protestant Reformation was carried out by both magisterial and nonmagisterial Reformers. The magisterial Reformers were those who used the offices of the state—or the magistrate—to bring doctrinal reform to the churches.[1] Furthermore, the magisterial Reformers, in both their Lutheran and Reformed varieties,

---

[1] This was the case because political jurisdiction overlapped with ecclesiastical jurisdiction (with exceptions for groups like immigrants or Jews).

began movements within established state churches. That meant that an individual's political citizenship normally entailed membership in the established church as well. But once the true gospel of justification by grace alone through faith alone in Christ alone was recovered, forces were unleashed which acted to undermine the whole concept of a legally established church.

If participating in the ordinances was not saving in and of itself, a baptized communicant could remain unbelieving and unsaved. This dawning realization brought about more concern for the salvation of the individual. The nature of evangelism and missions moved from incorporating individuals into the community through ritual and education, as much Roman Catholic mission work had done, to persuading and calling for a deliberate commitment by the individual. Eventually, nonmagisterial groups like the Anabaptists covenanted together to form congregations not necessarily sanctioned by the state. Indeed they were often illegal. Yet even in legally sanctioned Protestant churches, sermons were used to exhort the gathered to examine themselves to make their own calling and election sure.

The local church is more than a congregation, a gathering, but it is never less. While the New Testament refers to a plural number of leaders in a single congregation (e.g., Acts 20:17), never does it refer to multiple meetings as constituting a single local church. Furthermore, the idea that there can be one bishop or presbytery with authority over various congregations is the essence of either an Episcopalian or Presbyterian understanding of church polity; it is the opposite of congregationalism, which understands that each gathering that has preaching and the administration of baptism and the Lord's Supper has been given the keys of authority by Christ and should therefore have its own leadership, accountable under God only to the gathered church.

In recent decades a new question—or, better put, an old question in a new form—has arisen: May congregations rightly be considered a church with a single government and yet, by design, not regularly gather together? This is the question posed by both multisite and multiservice churches, and it effectively calls into question the meaning of the word *church*. For instance one author wrote, "A multi-site church shares a common vision, budget, leadership, and board."[2] But is a common vision, budget, leadership, and board sufficient to constitute a "church"? Notice that the element of gathering is absent from this definition. In what sense can it be a "church" if it never gathers together? Can a pastor or group of elders giving leadership to multiple campuses or sites rightly consider those different sites a single church? Can their collection of congregations be considered one congregation, one church? Most importantly, are multiservice[3] or multisite congregations biblical?[4]

On one level the question is settled lexically by simply considering the meaning of the word *ekklesia*. The New Testament authors regularly use the word to mean "assembly." This is highlighted by the fact that the word is used for more than just Christian assemblies. In Acts 7:38, Stephen referred to the congregation before Moses and the Lord at Mount Sinai as an *ekklesia*. And in Acts 19:32, Luke used the word to refer to a confused and violent assembly of people in the Ephesian amphitheatre who were intending to persecute the Christians. From these simple considerations it is clear that what these two usages have in common with a Christian "church" is that these groups, like Christians, gather. That's essential to their identity as a group.

But there is more to the question than one merely of normal usage. The physical gathering of the church presents a theological reality. The refractions of God's image in thousands of cultures and races and millions upon millions of individuals is presented, however partially and imperfectly,

---

[2] Geoff Surratt et al., eds., *Multi-site Church Revolution: Being One Church in Many Locations* (Grand Rapids: Zondervan, 2006), 18.

[3] I'm using the term multiservice—not in the sense of the whole congregation gathering *more* than once, such as at 9:00 a.m. and again at 6:00 p.m., but in the sense of meetings at which only a part of the church's membership is meeting as if it were the whole church. This is the case when churches offer multiple services, such as a 9:00 a.m. and an 11:00 a.m. service and encourages members to pick one service to attend.

[4] For a thorough yet gracious critique, see Thomas White and John M. Yeats, *Franchising McChurch: Feeding Our Obsession with Easy Christianity* (Colorado Springs, CO: David C. Cook, 2009).

in the weekly meeting. The visual witness of the diversity of
the body of Christ united together is celebrated by the elders
in heaven who sing to the Lamb, "with your blood you purchased men for God from every tribe and language and people and nation" (Rev 5:9). What John saw in his vision—"a
great multitude that no one could count, from every nation,
tribe, people and language, standing before the throne and
in front of the Lamb" (Rev 7:9)—is publicly though partially
seen weekly as Christians congregate together. In other
words the visible gathering constitutes a significant part
of the local church's eschatalogical witness. The picture of
people assembling in one place for worship points the world
to this marvelous end-of-history congregation.

Divisions should not lightly be introduced into a local
church. Language, distance, and even size are legitimate
reasons to establish separate congregations. But then each
separate congregation must uniquely represent the unity of
Christ's end-time assembly, and nothing should be encouraged which would obscure that witness—a witness of holiness and love, yes, but also of actual togetherness across
lines of income, ethnicity, class, and more.

As churches have reduced worship to evangelism, they
have begun to risk introducing divisions among these kinds
of groups. They have adopted actions appropriate for evangelism (like targeting certain groups such as the old or young,
the upper class or the artsy class, the rock-music or country-
music listeners) as an excuse to "narrow" their congregations by dividing them along worldly lines. Yet these are the
kinds of divisions which we must not introduce to Christ's
body, just as it would not be right to try representing the
reconciling gospel of Jesus Christ with services that are only
for non-Jews or caucasians. A part of a congregation, especially a part that shares some kind of worldly unifying char-
acteristic like age or ethnicity or hobbies, is not the whole.
It's no witness to the unifying power of the gospel. "And if
you greet only your brothers, what are you doing more than
others? Do not even pagans do that?" (Matt 5:47).

Such subgroups acting as complete congregations
divide the church wrongly. In the New Testament Jewish

and Gentile believers were not to have separate congregations. Indeed, their togetherness helped to display the gospel
they proclaimed (see Eph 2:11–22). The same is true today.
Churches that submerge differences of age, race, status,
background, or employment give witness to the power of the
gospel. Neither youth group meetings nor denominations
scattered across a whole continent are—in a strictly biblical sense—a church. Nor are the leaders considered alone.
A biblically ordered church regularly gathers the whole
congregation.[5]

No bishop or pastor, eldership or vision statement, budget or building shared among a number of different meetings constitutes a single church. While a local church may
have any of these things, it need not have any of them. And
yet, without regularly meeting together, it ceases to be a biblically ordered church. It may be true in that the gospel is
preached, but it is irregular in the sense that it is not according to the rule of Scripture.

Certainly a church is more than an assembly, but to
use *church* for anything *less* than an assembly would mean
substituting the part (e.g., leadership, budget, vision) for
the whole, with all the distortions that follow. The spiritual reality would be further hidden, including the spiritual
unity which becomes visible in the regular physical union
churches are called to enjoy in their local assemblies. In
this united meeting churches present a preview of one of
the glories of heaven—a preview that can only be distorted
by "congregations" that never congregate. Furthermore, the
united meeting also facilitates other aspects of the church's
unity—its Christlike love, its service and corporate worship
and outreach, all "so that the body of Christ may be built up
until we all reach unity in the faith and in the knowledge of
the Son of God and become mature, attaining to the whole
measure of the fullness of Christ" (Eph 4:12–13).

What about local churches that decide to forego meeting
together weekly but instead hold a variety of times or locations in which subgroups of the whole congregation meet

---

[5] With occasional absences as well, of course.

together? Such a formula at least raises serious questions.[6]
While a single congregation may meet *more* than once a
week (e.g., by gathering a second time on Sunday evening
or for a midweek meeting), it's difficult to see how they
could do anything *less*. Christians have always met together
weekly, even in the Scriptures. The fourth commandment
established a weekly rhythm among God's people,[7] and whatever the relation of the Old Testament Sabbath to the New
Testament Lord's Day, the nature of Christian obedience
always demanded that believers regularly assemble. It is not
surprising that the New Testament churches apparently met
at least weekly (if not more) and even began referring to the
"Lord's day" (Acts 20:7; 1 Cor 16:2; Rev 1:10; cf. Acts 2:46).
Preaching in the Bible presumes a gathered audience (e.g.,
Ezekiel's vision of the valley of dry bones in Ezekiel 37). So
does celebrating the Lord's Supper. And the kind of discipline
enjoined in Matthew 18 and mentioned in 2 Corinthians 2
certainly assumes the congregation assembles together.
Christians grow in love and care best by meeting together
regularly. Therefore, Heb 10:25 exhorts believers, "Let us not
give up meeting together, as some are in the habit of doing."

This weekly gathering also characterized the early
church. The non-Christian Roman official Pliny, writing to
Emperor Trajan about the year 112, referred to the fact that
Christians met regularly before daybreak on the appointed
day.[8] *The Didache*, an early second-century document,

---

[6] W. B. Johnson, the first president of the Southern Baptist Convention, made an
observation that, though it may seem controversial today, was taken for granted
when it was made and for a century afterwards: "The term church indicates one
church, one body of the Lord's people, meeting together in one place, and not
several congregations, forming one church" (Johnson, "The Gospel Developed,"
in *Polity: Biblical Arguments on How to Conduct Church Life*, ed. Mark Dever
[Washington, DC: Center for Church Reform, 2001], 171).
[7] "The primary reason for [Sunday worship's] origin must be the Christian need for
a time of distinctively Christian worship. The need for *some* regular time of worship must be clearly distinguished from possible reasons for the choice of *Sunday*
rather than another day. The choice of a day *of the week* is entirely natural in a
Jewish context and anything less frequent would surely not have met the need. . . .
It was the need for a regular and frequent time of Christian worship that led to the
choice of a day *of the week*" (R. J. Bauckham, "The Lord's Day," in *From Sabbath to
Lord's Day*, ed., D. A. Carson [Grand Rapids: Zondervan, 1982], 238).
[8] Pliny, Epistle X.xcvi, quoted in Henry Bettenson, ed., *Documents of the Christian
Church* (Oxford: Oxford University Press, 1943), 4.

exhorted Christians: "On the Lord's day assemble."[9] Justin Martyr, writing in the middle of the second century, described a common assembly on the first day of each week in which Christians came together for reading Scripture, preaching, prayer, and collecting an offering.[10] Hippolytus in the early third century referred to the pastor being chosen by all the people and assumed that God's people assembled each Lord's day.[11] Questions about the legitimacy of the Lord's Supper regularly turned on whether the bishop/pastor was present. From the church's earliest days, Christians have congregated regularly in local assemblies and have done so in obedience to God.[12]

Christians gather regularly for practical reasons: to hear God's Word read and preached, to witness faith professed in baptism and to take the Lord's Supper, to pray and sing together, to teach and give, to encourage one another, to bear one another's burdens and sorrows, and to know and be known. All of these aspects of a congregation's life are made possible or at least greatly helped by the congregational gathering. A congregation's united action is fostered by receiving the same teaching and having the same shaping experiences in public worship. In short, unity inside the congregation is easier to maintain when the congregation regularly gathers.[13]

Congregations are not formed merely by people gathering together but by their beliefs and commitments. An individual must decide to join a congregation, and then he or she must make the continual decision to participate through attendance, prayer, acts of service, financial support, and submission to the leadership of the elders and finally to the discipline of the congregation.[14] That's why

---

[9] *Didache*, XIV.

[10] Justin Martyr, *Apology*, I.lxvi.

[11] Hippolytus, *Apostolic Tradition*, I.ii.

[12] See W. B. Johnson, "Gospel Developed," 235–36.

[13] Is it fair to wonder if the popularity of multisite churches unintentionally encourages Christians to consumerism and passivity, viewing their church as simply a service provider rather than as a family gathering to work, learn, love, and serve together?

[14] Ultimately, of course, the church is gathered by the action of God's Spirit. As Luke wrote of the early church, "And the Lord added to their number daily those

Peter commanded people, "Repent and be baptized" (Acts 2:38). Those who are truly saved have repented of their sins and trusted in Christ.

At the same time, a Christian must publicly express the decision to repent and believe by publicly declaring his or her faith and covenanting together with a specific congregation of Christians. The congregation also must affirm the credibility of an individual's profession of faith.[15] It is not merely the decision of an individual to join or leave a church; rather, the decision to join or leave a church requires mutual consent between the individual and the congregation (other than by death).[16] Churches exist, in other words, as Christians gather together to proclaim and hear God's Word and then to affirm one another in the faith. A biblically faithful church is a gathered church.

---

who were being saved" (Acts 2:47). Yet God is not the only one at work in the local church. This divine action is met with a human response. As the New Hampshire Confession puts it, repentance and belief are the "inseparable graces wrought in our heart by the Holy Spirit of God" (Article 8).

[15] See Jonathan Leeman, *Church Membership: How the World Knows Who Represents Jesus* (Wheaton, IL: Crossway, 2012).

[16] This seems to be clearly implied in Paul's words to the Corinthians in 2 Cor 2:6–7. For more on this, see Jonathan Leeman, *Church Discipline: How the Church Protects the Name of Jesus* (Wheaton, IL: Crossway, 2012).

14

A Congregational Church: Putting Together the Structure of the Church

Nowhere does the Bible prescribe a polity for the universal church, that body of all Christians everywhere. The only other definition for *church* in the New Testament is of the local assembly. While no church constitution is included in the New Testament documents, the Bible has principles which inform a congregation's life. And the New Testament has explicit teachings on church structure. Both the officers and polity described in the New Testament have led many Christians to conclude that the church should be structured congregationally. This has implications for how one congregation relates to other congregations and to other connections of Christians outside their number. And it has implications for how leadership is exercised within the congregation.

Local and Universal

A congregational church recognizes the congregation as the final earthly court of appeal in matters of dispute. Members' meetings are held where decisions are made by voting. Naturally, a higher degree of consensus is needed than in churches of other polities. More responsibility rests on each member, and more authority resides in them. As Jonathan Leeman argued so carefully and clearly, "Even with all its imperfections, the church represents Jesus on earth."[1]

Relations Between Congregations

Such congregations have sometimes been called "independent" as opposed to "connectionalist," like Presbyterian or Episcopalian churches. Congregationalist churches are not, however, independent of one another in affection, care, advice, or cooperation. Both in Scripture and in history, congregations have cultivated care and concern for one another. In the New Testament period, collections were taken and given, missionaries and teachers were sent, and recommendations and cautions were shared between congregations. This pattern has repeated itself among Anabaptist and Baptist congregations, as well as among many other congregational churches.

Traditionally, Baptists have used associations between churches to help ministers and congregations take counsel with one another, reach joint conclusions, stop controversies, and draw doctrinal boundaries. And congregations have freely come together to accomplish work that would generally exceed the resources of one congregation, such as ministerial education and missionary support. Congregational churches are in one narrow sense "independent," but in other ways they are more accurately described as voluntarily interdependent.

Denominational Relationships

Voluntary connections of congregations like the Southern Baptist Convention, the American Baptist Churches, and the National Baptist Convention long ago settled into the popular American consciousness as denominations. Many if not most other denominations are connectional churches where final

---

[1] Jonathan Leeman, *The Church and the Surprising Offense of God's Love* (Wheaton, IL: Crossway, 2010), 195.

decisions on matters of doctrine and discipline cannot be handled by the local assemblies but must be decided by regional, national, or even internationally recognized assemblies, courts, or bishops. However, denominations of congregational churches are far different from other denominations.[2]

One can speak in the singular of the Presbyterian Church in the United States of America or of the United Methodist Church in a way one could never correctly speak of the National Baptist Church or the Southern Baptist Church. While it is commonly understood what such expressions mean, they reveal an ignorance about the nature of the churches they mean to describe. Even if members of congregational churches sometimes exhibit great "tribal loyalty" to their denomination, they are actually only members of local churches which themselves in turn only voluntarily and never necessarily cooperate with regional and national bodies. Their congregations need not continue to affiliate with any particular convention in order to continue being a true church.

Congregationalism with Leadership

None of the aforesaid teaching on congregationalism should be mistaken as advocating leaderless anarchy in churches.[3] Recognizing the congregation as the final court of appeal for matters of dispute is hardly inimical to the exercise of authority within the church. And other noncongregational polities, including Presbyterian, Episcopalian, and even Roman Catholic, have demonstrated a certain inevitability of congregationalism by recognizing representative bodies at various levels and even by advising congregational assent for many decisions to be enacted.

Elder Led, Congregationally Governed

The most coherent way to understand the New Testament's presentation of local church polity is to recognize the role

---

[2] The Free Will Baptist tradition has a history of more connectionalism than most other Baptists in America. See J. Matthew Pinson, *Free Will Baptists & Church Government* (Nashville: National Association of Free Will Baptists, 2008).
[3] Stanton Norman wrestled with the current Southern Baptist tension between congregationalism and leadership in his book, *The Baptist Way: Distinctives of a Baptist Church* (Nashville: B&H, 2005), 101–10.

of both individual leaders and the congregation as a whole.[4] Some recommend a pastor should govern the church almost like a CEO. But this gives inadequate attention to Scripture's teaching on both the plurality of elders and the role of the whole congregation. Others recommend the church should be governed by elders. This position is rightly distinguished from Presbyterianism because it does not simultaneously envision submitting to a hierarchy of authority outside the local congregation's body of elders. But while this position helpfully discerns what the New Testament says about a plurality of elders, it also discounts the scriptural evidence for both congregational responsibility and the special recognition of a lead teaching elder, like Timothy in Ephesus—what might today be described as a "senior pastor." Still others recommend a vigorous congregationalism that is exercised at the expense of any other authority, whether corporate (a plurality of elders) or individual (a lead pastor).

Too often these varieties of congregationalism are pitted against one another.[5] But all three aspects of authority seen in the New Testament (individual, plural eldership, and congregational) should be enjoyed in every congregation. One elder supported by the church and responsible for the ministry of the Word could well be recognized as having a senior position in order to give leadership to the church's vision and direction. At the same time, a plurality of elders, whether paid or unpaid, can together lead the congregation in matters of doctrine and discipline. And at the same time, the congregation can, in humility, shoulder the responsibility for acting as the final court, under God, in all matters of discipline and doctrine which rise to that level of significance. Which matters are dealt with at what level may vary from congregation to congregation. Of course, this congregational authority seems to be merely authority to affirm or deny the assertion of teaching (or teachers) and of members,

---

[4] See Phil Newton, *Elders in Congregational Life: Rediscovering the Biblical Model for Church Leadership* (Grand Rapids: Kregel, 2005); Benjamin L. Merkle, *Why Elders? A Biblical and Practical Guide for Church Members* (Grand Rapids: Kregel, 2009); Daniel Evans and Joseph Godwin Jr., *Elder Governance: Insights into Making the Transition* (Eugene, OR: Resource Publications, 2011).

[5] E.g., Brand and Norman, *Perspectives on Church Government.*

not to lead. The congregation is not in competition with the elders. The congregation's authority is more like an emergency brake than a steering wheel. The congregation more normally recognizes than creates, responds rather than initiates, confirms rather than proposes.

The New Testament teaches the significance of congregational assent for what must be taught and believed (e.g., Gal 1:6–9) and for who is admitted and dismissed from membership (e.g., 1 Corinthians 5; 2 Cor 2:6–7). The local assembly bears final (though not sole) responsibility for these two crucial aspects of the church, the teaching and the membership. In fact, it is by congregations so judging teaching and members that they exercise the keys Christ has entrusted to his church (see Matt 16:19; 18:17).[6]

In Matthew 16, Jesus authorized the apostolic church to affirm or deny professions of faith (e.g., who is Jesus?), and in Matthew 18 Jesus authorized the church to affirm or deny how such a profession is lived out (e.g., will a sinner repent?). Galatians 1:6–9 speaks of the church judging doctrine, even as 1 Corinthians 5 is a call to the church to judge the life which is to validate the profession.

For all of its authority, the local congregation has no authority to delegate the keys to another group. It may go outside itself for counsel and advice, but the ultimate responsibility for determining teaching or membership in the local church may not be outsourced to any body outside of itself. Any such delegation by the congregation undermines its claims to be a biblically ordered church.[7] The New Testament's teaching on the nature of the congregation and the role of its leaders clearly indicates that a biblically faithful church is a congregational church.

---

[6] For further reflection on "the keys," see Jonathan Leeman, *The Church and the Surprising Offense of God's Love*, chap. 4.

[7] One obvious qualification of this statement is that times of a church's beginning and ending may well bring with it exceptional circumstances which call for temporary measures in which one or more of these aspects of leadership are not yet fully realized.

15

A Baptist Church: Should We Have Baptist Churches Today?

A t the heart of church membership is regular communing together at the Lord's Supper. Those who are regularly welcomed to that table are essentially a church's members. They are those who are self-examined (1 Cor 11:28) and also examined by others (that is, by those who have not been excluded as an act of discipline). Being baptized is part of the obedience that would be expected for one to come to the table.[1] Thus Baptists have traditionally thought that baptism is "a prerequisite to other rights and responsibilities in the church, including participation in the Lord's Supper."[2] As John Gill put it, "After the ordinance of baptism, follows

---

[1] D. Broughton Knox, relying on Paul's statement in 1 Cor 1:17, denied that New Testament baptism was important for those brought up in Christian homes. Advocating infant baptism, Knox wrote: "It is not identical with the baptism of holy scripture, which was a baptism of repentance with a view to forgiveness. Such a baptism does not fit the circumstances of a Christian family. . . . To confess Christ by being immersed under water is only practiced because it is believed that Jesus sent us to baptize with water. But, as Paul makes clear, this is not the case" (*Selected Works*, vol. 2 [Youngston, OH: Matthias Media, 2003], 308–9).

[2] Charles Kelley Jr., Richard Land, R. Albert Mohler Jr., *The Baptist Faith and Message* (Nashville: LifeWay, 2007), 97. See John Hammett, "Baptism and the Lord's Supper" in *The Baptist Faith and Message 2000*, ed. Douglas K. Blount and Joseph D. Woodell (Lanham, MD: Rowan & Littleton, 2007), 75. That this is what Southern Baptists have traditionally and officially believed, see The New Hampshire Confession, Article XIV, and The Baptist Faith and Message, Article 7.

the ordinance of the Lord's Supper; the one is preparatory to the other; and he that has a right to the one has a right to the other; and none but such who have submitted to the former, ought to be admitted to the latter."[3]

In the New Testament we have no record of anyone taking the Lord's Supper who had not first been baptized. The sign of union with Christ—baptism—precedes the sign of communion together. In Christ's Great Commission, baptism is mentioned before "teaching them to obey everything" that Christ commanded. It is clearly intended to be an initial step in discipleship. This also fits with the analogy from the relationship of circumcision to the Passover in the Old Testament. No uncircumcised male was to take the Passover meal. So only those who are baptized are to take the Lord's Supper.[4]

How should such biblical truth affect the practice of the local church? Should churches take as members those who have not been baptized?[5] These are pressing questions for this generation. If agreement on a particular matter is not essential for salvation, should agreement be regarded as essential for church membership? If the question springs from a receding grasp on the truth or at least a declining willingness to define and defend the truth—a mere essentialism—then more basic and dangerous issues than a misunderstanding of baptism are at stake. If, on the other hand, the question emerges from a sincere desire for the unity of the body of Christ, then the question is a noble one and deserves serious consideration. Christians from John

---

[3] John Gill, *A Complete Body of Doctrinal and Practical Divinity* (1839; repr., Paris, AR: The Baptist Standard Bearer, n.d.), 915.

[4] The implication of differing understandings of baptism means reduced fellowship between Christians of otherwise similar convictions. Since no one has questioned the validity of believer's baptism, it has always been the believer Baptists who have been left in the difficult position of not recognizing the baptisms of Christians coming from paedo-Baptist churches. Many defenses of Baptists against the charge of being bigots on this point have been written. One that is both a classic and typical is Abraham Booth, *A Defense for the Baptists* (1778; repr., Paris, AR: The Baptist Standard Bearer, 2006).

[5] A good, simple work on this topic is Bill James, *Baptism and Church Membership* (Darlington, England: Reformation Today Trust, 2006). Another contemporary defense of having Baptist churches is chap. 4 of John S. Hammett, *Biblical Foundations for Baptist Churches: A Contemporary Ecclesiology* (Grand Rapids: Kregel, 2005).

Bunyan to D. Martyn Lloyd-Jones have pled for liberty on this point. They have advocated that agreement on the legitimacy or illegitimacy of infant baptism not be required for church membership.[6]

This position of neutrality over a matter not essential for salvation is gaining in popularity. The question essentially is, or at least very nearly is, Should we continue to have Baptist churches? If the question is posed as one of love versus dogmatism, the answer is easy, but the real issues at stake may be obscured. Two matters in particular cannot be overlooked.

First, some things are not essential for an individual's salvation, yet agreement on them is essential in order for a church to function. One thinks of questions surrounding church government, qualifications for membership, or women serving as pastors and elders. Such issues of polity and practice may be declared "matters indifferent," and freedom may be allowed among different congregations for determining their own answers to these questions. But finally, each congregation must do one thing and not the other. A congregation either recognizes women as elders or it does not, an outside bishop as an authority or not, and infants as viable subjects of baptism or not.

This brings us to the second and more important matter which must not be overlooked—fidelity to Scripture. If baptism is not essential for Communion and church membership, it effectively becomes a matter of individual judgment. The desire for doctrinal inclusiveness and unity in the Spirit ironically reduces obedience to a matter of subjective preference. Some, like John Bunyan, have argued that disobedience to a command of Christ, especially when done in ignorance, represents a mere lack of light to be borne with more than it represents a disciplinable offense or a sin.

A sin can consist of either an action or an intention. Certainly the intention to disobey God is sin. But a disobedient action toward God is also a sin even if the individual does

---

[6] The controversies about terms of admission to communion among nineteenth-century Baptists provide a rich resource for more biblical thinking on these matters. For example, see R. B. C. Howell, *Terms of Communion*.

not intend to sin. The Bible teaches clearly that there are unintentional sins.[7] Intentions are an important consideration in the nature and gravity of a sin, but they are not the only consideration. One of the effects of sin is to stupefy the sinner, to dull and darken the faculties. So those dwelling in sin are said to dwell in darkness, but that darkness does not ameliorate one's guilt. In the parable of the sheep and the goats (Matthew 25), Jesus taught with stark clarity that obedience to God does not lie in the eye of the beholder, unless the beholder is God himself. Many goats thought they had lived righteous lives, but Jesus said they have not.

How then do we know what God considers obedience? By his own self-revelation. There is no other sure and certain guide! If Christ has commanded Christians to be baptized, then countermanding that instruction, or substituting mere intention, even sincere intention, does not serve him best.

Christ's glory is most displayed in the church when baptism guards both the regeneracy of church membership and the consistency of the church's corporate witness. If we understand that Christ commands the church to baptize only those who believe, then it seems clear that a biblically faithful church is a Baptist church.

---

[7] E.g., Leviticus 4–5; Numbers 15; Ezekiel 45.

Conclusion: Why Does This Matter?

What significance does a right ecclesiology have for the church today? A right ecclesiology matters for the church's leadership, membership, structure, culture, and even character. Ultimately, a right ecclesiology touches on God's glory itself. The church is not only an institution founded by Christ; it is also his body. In it is reflected God's own glory. How will theology, the Bible, and even God himself be known apart from the church? What community will understand and explain God's creation and providence to the world? How will the ravages of sin be explained, the person and work of Christ extolled, the Spirit's saving work seen, and the return of Christ proclaimed to coming generations if not by the church? The theology expounded in every chapter of this book presses outward to be known, and it presses outward through the church. Therefore, getting the doctrine of the church right becomes a benefit to people, as the truth about God and his world is more correctly known, taught, and modeled.

This Matters for the Church's Leadership

Centrality of Preaching in Our Churches

Pastors in churches today must recover the understanding that their primary role is to preach the Word of God. This must happen both for the sake of the flock and for the sake of reaching those outside the flock.

The purpose of preaching God's Word to God's people is to build up, or edify, the church, which is God's will for the church. Whether or not numerical growth results from biblical preaching in any given congregation at any given time, Christ's church will experience true growth and edification through teaching and instruction. To this end pastors must also lead the church toward a recovery of corrective church discipline. This is accomplished only when the leadership itself understands the Bible's teaching about the church and then gives itself to patiently teaching the congregation in these matters.

Whenever pastors recover the centrality of preaching in their ministry, beneficial effects follow. Congregations are better fed and healthier, and then they become better witnesses in their communities. Too often leaders promote church growth exclusively through evangelism, but they fail to consider that an untaught and unhealthy church is a poor witness. And a poor church witness undermines the evangelistic ministries of the congregation. The pastor who recommits himself to feeding the congregation well best prepares his congregation for evangelism and growth. Healthy organisms naturally grow.

The Importance of Believer's Baptism and Believer's Communion

God's Spirit creates believers through the preaching and hearing of the Word, yet God also intends for those believers to be collected together in congregations that are pure and protected. To this end pastors must take greater care both in scrutinizing candidates for baptism and in encouraging the congregation to scrutinize themselves before partaking of the Lord's Supper. If baptism functions as the watery moat separating church and world, and if the Lord's Supper manifests the ongoing appearance of the church, then pastors today must recover the sense of gravity each ordinance requires.

Hebrews 13:17 promises that leaders will give an account for those under their charge. Will today's leaders give an account for carelessly admitting wolves into baptism or the Lord's Supper? Will the condemnations heaped on Israel's shepherds in Ezekiel 34 be repeated on undershepherds of the church today who have left Christ's sheep to wander scattered and unprotected? The leaders of our congregations must remember that the right preaching of God's Word and the right administration of baptism and the Lord's Supper form the basic calling of their lives.

This Matters for the Church's Membership

A right ecclesiology also has implications for the church's membership.[1] Therefore, the reasons and requirements for membership should be widely and clearly understood.

Why Join a Church?

Most evangelical Christians today seem to treat their church as one more thing to help out their Christian life, perhaps along with this Bible study, that music, those authors, this retreat, and keeping a journal. In other words the Christian conceives of his or her spiritual life as fundamentally one's own business, managed by selecting among various helps. This approach contrasts with an older and more biblical way of thinking about the Christian life that is congregationally shaped, where the demands of the gospel are made concrete in a particular local church (see 1 John 4:20).

Being a member of a local church should be made to seem normal for Christians. Lives lived in regular love, fellowship,

---

[1] If this were widely understood among the members, congregations would be able to consider carefully the delicate question of the relation of children of church members to the church.

and accountability make the gospel clear to the world. Jesus said that Christians' love for one another would enable the world to recognize Christians as those who follow Christ (John 13:34–35). In that sense a vigorous practice of church membership helps a congregation's evangelism. It also helps Christians gain a proper assurance of their own salvation. As Christians observe, teach, encourage, and rebuke one another, the local church begins to act as a cooperative that corroborates assurance of salvation. Church membership is good for weak Christians because it bring them into a place of feeding and accountability. Church membership is good for strong Christians because it enables them to provide an example for what a true Christian life is like.[2]

Committed church membership is also good for the leaders of the church. How will God's work go forward if Christians do not organize together to serve him? And how will Christians receive the gifts God gives them in their leaders if there is no flock marked out for those leaders to steward? Finally, practicing church membership glorifies God. As Christians gather together to form the body of Christ, his character is reflected and expressed. Recovering this understanding of church membership should be one of the chief desires of congregations today.[3]

Before one quickly points to the parachurch as accomplishing the same objectives, remember that the parachurch neither has the same commitment to systematically proclaiming the whole counsel of God, nor does it have the mechanisms of baptism, the Lord's Supper, and church discipline for drawing a clear, bright line that says to the world, "Here are the people of God." The parachurch is and always intends to be a particular subset of the church centered on a

---

[2] For more on why a believer should join a church, see Jim Samra, *The Gift of Church* (Grand Rapids: Zondervan, 2010).
[3] For more on this, see Mark Dever, *Nine Marks of a Healthy Church,* 2nd ed. (Wheaton, IL: Crossway, 2004); also Mark Dever, *A Display of God's Glory* (Washington, DC: 9Marks, 2001); Mark Dever, "Regaining Meaningful Membership," in *Restoring Integrity in Baptist Churches*, ed. Thomas White, Jason Duesing, and Malcolm Yarnell (Grand Rapids: Kregel, 2008), 45–61.

shared task. As Byron Straughn put it, the parachurch is like our soccer team, but the church is like our family.[4]

Requirements

The idea that membership in a local church should only require a profession of faith in Christ is an idea that is both common and destructive to the life and witness of the church. Historically, Baptists have realized that any profession of faith should be tried and deemed as credible. After all, a saving profession of faith includes repentance. A Christian life will be revealed not only by participation in baptism and the Lord's Supper but also by regular attendance at the congregation's gatherings and a submission to the discipline of the congregation. This includes regularly praying for the congregation and tithing. Every congregation has the responsibility for deciding what membership standards are appropriate for its own church.[5]

Relation of Children to the Church

One of the areas in most need of reexamination in today's churches is the relation of the children of church members to the church. In non-Baptist Protestant congregations this relationship begins with infant baptism and is usually completed by confirmation around age 12. In Baptist churches traditionally children were recognized as having an important role. They were regarded as the objects of all natural affections, but they were also recognized as specially entrusted to Christian families for training in the Lord. Conversions could occur at early ages, of course, but it was generally thought most wise to delay baptism until maturity tested the reality of their conversion.[6] Earlier

---

[4] See Byron Straughn, "For the Parachurch: Know the Difference Between Families and Soccer Teams," http://www.9marks.org/ejournal/parachurch-know-difference-between-families-soccer-teams, accessed 28 July 2011.

[5] A helpful guide for this is Thabiti Anyabwile, *What Is a Healthy Church Member?* (Wheaton, IL: Crossway, 2008). Anyabwile explained that a healthy church member is an expositional listener, a biblical theologian, gospel saturated, genuinely converted, a biblical evangelist, a committed member, seeks discipline, a growing disciple, a humble follower, and a prayer warrior.

[6] Much historical work remains to be done in this area, but the following facts are suggestive. Consider the noted Baptist ministers of the eighteenth and nineteenth

Baptists understood that time is necessary for seeing a Christian profession lived out, especially in those who are not yet mature.[7] Many Christians in antiquity and around the world today regularly practice a period of waiting after profession as a means of evidencing the reality of the person's profession.[8] There seems to be little doubt that, at least in Southern Baptist churches, the last century has seen an increase in nominalism while the average age of baptism has been decreasing. It seems likely the two statistics are related.

Moreover, concerns with false baptisms (leading to a growing number of rebaptisms) should not be limited to the adverse effects a local church bears when pagans are

---

centuries. John Gill was brought up in a Baptist home and was baptized at age 19 in 1716 (just three weeks shy of his twentieth birthday). Samuel Medley was brought up in a Baptist home and was baptized at age 22 in December 1760. Richard Furman was brought up in a non-Christian home and was baptized at age 17 in 1772. John Dagg was baptized in Middleburg, Virginia, at age 18 in the spring of 1812. J. Newton Brown was baptized in Hudson, New York, at age 14 in 1817. J. M. Pendleton was baptized near Pembroke, Kentucky, at age 18 in 1829. P. H. Mell was brought up in a strong Christian home and was baptized at age 18 in 1832 (according to his biography by his son). J. R. Graves was brought up in a strong Christian home and was baptized at age 15 in 1835 (according to O. L. Hailey's biography). Sylvanus Dryden Phelps (author of the hymn "Something for Thee") was brought up in a Christian home and was baptized at age 22 in 1838 (according to Cathcart's *Baptist Encyclopedia*). John A. Broadus was brought up in a strong Christian home and was baptized at age 16 in 1843 (according to A. T. Robertson's biography). Charles Fenton James was baptized in 1864 at age 20 in the trenches near Petersburg, Virginia, while he was a Confederate soldier (see George B. Taylor, *Virginia Baptist Ministers*, 38). C. H. Spurgeon baptized his two sons when they were 18 (see Dallimore, *Spurgeon*, 181). John R. Sampey was brought up in a Christian home and was baptized at age 13 in 1877 (according to his *Memoirs*, 7). He had already worked on his father's farm. E. Y. Mullins was brought up in the home of a Baptist minister in Texas and was baptized at age 20 in 1880. The above pastors all had jobs by the time they were baptized. H. Wheeler Robinson was brought up by a Christian mother in Northampton, England, and was baptized at age 16 in 1888.

This delay is still typical among most Baptists in Africa, Europe, and elsewhere overseas. E.g., consider the practice in France: "Positioned in the middle of the service, it [baptism] serves as the centerpiece of worship. Baptism in France tends to come at a later age—sixteen is the youngest—and candidates always testify in the service before being baptized. While these traditions and practices seem a bit strange, the result is a vibrant and dynamic faith that puts Baptists on the cutting edge of the evangelical movement in France and Europe" (C. Frank Thomas in *Why I Am a Baptist*, ed. Cecil P. Staton Jr. [Macon, GA: Smyth & Helwys, 1999], 170).

[7] See Dennis Gunderson, *Your Child's Profession of Faith* (Amityville, NY: Calvary, 1994); and Jim Eliff, *Childhood Conversions* (Parkville: Christian Communicators Worldwide, 1997).

[8] See Hippolytus, *On the Apostolic Tradition*, trans. Alistair Stewart-Sykes (Crestwood, NY: SVS Press, 2001), 103.

welcomed into membership and called saints, as serious as those effects are.[9] The effects borne throughout eternity by pastors and churches who give false assurance of salvation to unbelievers are grave and discourage haste. In some cases there is a great need for wisdom to balance between the sometimes competing interests of encouragement and healthy caution.

This Matters for the Church's Structure

A right doctrine of the church should affect not only a church's leadership and membership; it should also affect its structure.

The Need for Both Clear Leadership and Congregational Responsibility

Too many in the last generation have derided authority. Authority may well be, as one book title suggested a few years ago, "the most misunderstood idea in America." "Americans do not distinguish authority, which is something good, from authoritarianism, which is something bad."[10] A suspicion of all power because of the abuse of some power holders has created a whole strain of misshapen Christian piety in which the powerlessness of Christ on the cross is viewed as the sole paradigm for all who exercise authority. While humility should inhere in all Christian exercise of authority, God has also placed leaders within the body to teach, give direction and guidance, be examples, and make decisions.[11] Exercising trust in almost every sphere, whether marriage, family, work, the state, or the church, is for the Christian ultimately a reflection of trust in God.

Denominational battles within the Southern Baptist Convention in the last century have spawned a virulent strain of novel and naïve Baptist history which suggests it

---

[9] See P. B. Jones, et al., "A Study of Adults Baptized in Southern Baptist Churches, 1993," *Research Report*, January 1995 (Atlanta: Home Mission Board).
[10] Eugene Kennedy and Sara Charles, *Authority: The Most Misunderstood Idea in America* (New York, Free Press, 1997), 1.
[11] C. J. Mahaney, *Humility: True Greatness* (Sisters, OR: Multnomah, 2005) is an excellent resource to consider the nature and cultivation of the Christlike humility that should mark the church and its ministers.

is the essence of Baptist identity to be individualistic, cantankerous, and divisive. The rich Protestant doctrine of the priesthood of all believers,[12] originally formulated to oppose a mediatorial class of ordained Roman Catholic priests, has been transfigured into the optimistic and simplistic early twentieth-century phrase (by E. Y. Mullins) "soul competency." A biblically faithful stress on the sole mediatorship of Christ (the Reformation emphasis) has been traded (wittingly?) for a mistaken defense of human ability.

At best the idea of soul competency simply restates one implication of the fact that humans are created in the image of God—that we are made spiritual beings who are able to have a relationship with God. At worst the idea degenerates into a semireligious humanism in which proclaiming Christ's work becomes unnecessary. Following in the train of this misused doctrine, every locus of theology is reshaped—from the atonement to the inspiration of Scripture. In ecclesiology it tends to undermine ideas of authority and leadership in the church. But leadership is a gift from God and should be received by churches as a gift. Rejecting leadership deprives the church of Christ's gift, impoverishes the body, and hinders the church in its life and work. The polity of the church is like the prongs of a ring which hold the precious treasure of the gospel—comparatively unimportant, its purpose and role is to secure that which is of most importance.

Three gospel-preaching congregations with differing polities (e.g., Episcopalian, Presbyterian, Congregational) may look the same when everything is going well. But if problems occur, their polities come out in living color. Differences are seen to be important, sometimes even vital—even to the point of determining whether or not a faithful gospel witness continues in that church. While no polity eliminates problems from a congregation, a carefully biblical structure which recognizes both the leadership of the elders and the responsibility of the congregation best protects the flock (Acts 20:28; 1 Pet 5:2) and encourages the leaders (Heb

[12] For an excellent treatment of this doctrine, see Timothy George, "The Priesthood of All Believers and the Quest for Theological Integrity," *CTR* 3, no. 2 (1989): 283–94.

13:17). While even the most biblically structured congregations will make mistakes, the nearer a church's polity gets
to recognizing the biblical responsibilities held by the elders
and by the congregation, the better protected and prepared
the congregation is for the storms that inevitably come to all
churches in this fallen world.

Gender Roles and Leadership in the Churches

One factor that has led many local congregations either
to adopt an elder-led model or to avoid such a model has been
the increasing controversy in popular culture over gender-
based distinctions. After all, the New Testament is relatively
clear on reserving the office of elder for men. But a society that has dismissed gender as an appropriate boundary
marker for marriage is a society that has long ago lost any
sense of gender roles in the church. Historically the church
took the New Testament's teaching on male eldership at
face value. But that position was slowly abandoned in twentieth-century America. In 1924, the Methodist Episcopal
church voted to ordain women. They were followed by the
main body of northern Presbyterians in 1956, and then the
Episcopalians in 1976, and finally the main Lutheran body
in 1979.[13] Among the new Pentecostal movements, Aimee
Semple McPherson, Kathryn Kuhlman, and other women
had prominent teaching ministries.

Among Baptist churches the movement toward female
ordination has been slower, but the process has undoubtedly
been aided by extrabiblical structures such as committees,
church councils, and staff positions, which are neither mandated nor described in Scripture, and which have, therefore,
been more easily filled with women—even in otherwise biblically conservative churches. Moving to a plurality of elders
brings clear biblical passages to bear on these issues, which
support male leadership in the congregation.[14]

---

[13] See Mark Noll, *A History of Christianity in the United States and Canada* (Grand
Rapids: Eerdmans, 1992), 513.
[14] See Grudem and Rainey, *Pastoral Leadership*. It should be noted that genuinely
biblical leadership is consensual, not coercive, and is concerned with guiding and
serving, not "lording it over" others in pride. Should more secularly conceived
questions of power be raised, it must be remembered that in most congregations

This Matters for the Church's Culture

Not only are matters of leadership, membership, and formal structure affected by a doctrine of the church, so too are matters of the church's culture.

Culture of Discipling in the Church

Along with the hard and defined skeletal structure of a church, there is also the more subtle, changeable, variable, and enveloping culture of a church. The culture of a church is constituted by the combination of peculiar expectations and practices which do not make the church a church but which do in fact typify a particular congregation. Suppose then that a congregation is marked by graciousness, a concern for truth, and a zeal for missions. These qualities are certainly appropriate and consistent with the scriptural presentation of a church, but they are not specifically required of every congregation in order to be recognized as a true church.

That said, the soundness of a church is greatly improved when the congregation cultivates a culture of discipleship and growth in which individual Christian growth is normal, not exceptional. One indicator of growth, moreover, is an increasing level of concern for the spiritual state of others. A concern for others should include non-Christians around the world (thus an emphasis on missions), in the congregation's own local area (thus an emphasis on evangelism), and especially for other members of the congregation (thus an emphasis on discipling one another). A culture of discipling, evangelism, and missions best encourages the church to be what God has made it to be—a reflection of his own character.

Churches receive God's grace, relish it, and reflect it to others. Congregations should note and repeat evidences of God's grace in one another's lives through testimonies and other public encouragements. Baptismal testimonies,

women comprise the majority of members, so women could organize as women (along with men who agreed with them) at any time and change their church's practice if they became convinced that the positions laid out in this chapter, and traditionally practiced by Christians, were in error.

thoughtful prayer requests, interviews during members meetings—these and many other ways can encourage the church in discipleship and make the atmosphere helpfully provocative for Christian growth.[15]

Current Challenge of Nominalism

Ranged against this radiant vision of the church is a large and growing nominalism in many evangelical churches today. Congregation after congregation is marked by membership roles filled with nonattending "members." Even among those members who do attend, too many live lives indistinct from the nonbelievers around them. This nominalism dulls and undercuts Christian evangelism; it pushes the church and individual Christians toward disillusionment, apathetic discouragement, or division; and ultimately it dishonors God.[16] Surely if this situation is to be addressed, the importance of the nature and life of the local church must be recovered. Evangelicals have advanced various answers to today's decline in churches. Space here permits a brief mention of only a few.

Spirit answer: Pentecostalism. Since the beginning of the twentieth century, the rise of Pentecostalism has arguably been the most significant sociological development in world Christianity. The Christian landscapes in Africa and

---

[15] A good course of study for local church leaders to understand and move toward this more organic view of the church would be the following four books, and in this order: Joseph Bayly, *The Gospel Blimp* (Chicago: David C. Cook, 2002); Robert Coleman, *The Master Plan of Evangelism* (Grand Rapids: Fleming H. Revell, 1963); Colin Marshal and Tony Payne, *The Trellis and the Vine* (Youngston, OH: Matthias Media, 2009); and Mark Dever and Paul Alexander, *The Deliberate Church* (Wheaton, IL: Crossway 2005).

[16] Surveying the state of the churches in the mid-nineteenth century, John L. Dagg wrote: "Much that has existed, and that now exists, among the professed followers of Christ, cannot be contemplated by one who sincerely loves him, without deep distress" (John L. Dagg, *A Treatise on Church Order* [Southern Baptist Publication Society, 1858], 11). A century and a half later, John Piper reflected on the disturbing state of many churches today: "The injustice and persecution and suffering and hellish realities in the world today are so many and so large and so close that I can't help but think that, deep inside, people are longing for something weighty and massive and rooted and stable and eternal. So it seems to me that the trifling with silly little sketches and breezy welcome-to-the-den styles on Sunday morning are just out of touch with what matters in life. . . . I doubt that a religious ethos with such a feel of entertainment can really survive as Christian for too many more decades" (*Counted Righteous in Christ* [Wheaton, IL: Crossway, 2002], 22–23).

South America have been transformed, and more established churches in Europe and North America have been affected. Many of these Christians think the answer to the church's problems lies in rediscovering the biblical teaching of the baptism of the Holy Spirit. Many Pentecostals say this experience, which includes speaking in unknown tongues, signifies conversion. Many newer charismatics say the baptism of the Holy Spirit is a second experience intended for every believer after conversion. They believe that Christians invigorated by this baptism would replace the lamentable and dull witness of too many Christians and their congregations.

Size answer: Every member/small group/house church. Other groups of Christians have suggested that the answer to nominal Christianity lies in recovering the dynamic of smaller groups, in which no function exists for inactive members. This has been variously advocated through the use of small groups, the cell church structure, and the house church movement.[17] Some have even advocated setting low quantitative limits on congregations, saying that anything beyond the set limit turns churches into mere "preaching points" and undermines the ability of the pastor to pastor as well as the ability of members to involve themselves meaningfully with other members in ministry.

Substitute   answer: Parachurch,   purpose-driven, homogenous, mission-centered. Still other Christians have given up on the traditional local and heterogeneous congregation. This despair or rejection can be observed in the growth philosophy that recommends forming whole congregations around a single vision statement. It is also seen in some "purpose-driven" models. The rejection of heterogeneity is even more pronounced in congregations that set their mission on one homogeneous group, whether defined ethnically, generationally, sociodemographically, or otherwise.[18] The homogeneous unit principle lies behind this

---

[17] Mark Dever, "The Priesthood of All Believers: Reconsidering Every Member Ministry," in *The Compromised Church*, ed. John H. Armstrong (Wheaton, IL: Crossway, 1998), 85–116.

[18] For a critique of one popular stream of homogeneity in churches, see Kevin DeYoung and Ted Kluck, *Why We're Not Emergent (By Two Guys Who Should Be)* (Chicago: Moody, 2008).

approach—the recognition that in mission settings like reaches like. Members of one caste in India, for example, have more difficulty reaching individuals from a different caste. Yet the homogeneous-unit principle has reordered the ecclesiology of many churches in the name of evangelism. Its logical conclusion is the rejection of the whole congregation in exchange for a missional parachurch subgroup, though they may continue referring to themselves as a church.[19]

So-long answer: Individualism. Still others who call themselves Christians have perceived the doleful state of many congregations and have concluded that the organized congregation should simply be rejected. This rejection can occur publicly, as with radio preacher Harold Camping's pronouncement that Christians should desert the churches because the church age has ended.[20] Or it can occur more quietly, as when individuals simply desist in church participation. Yet in both cases self-defined Christians emphasize something like Jesus' teaching on the heart or doctrines like justification by faith alone in order to justify their rejection of the congregation's role in the Christian life. In short, nominalism and hypocrisy in churches are used to justify noninvolvement.

Sales answer: excitement, give them what they want, pragmatism, marketing, consumerism. Others place the church's hope for recovery in recreating excitement. Many authors and pastors appeal to a convert's experience of newness, a historical church's experience in a time of revival, or even the young church in the book of Acts in order to argue the best way forward is to replicate such excitement. While specific diagnoses of problems vary, most solutions tend toward a "give them what they want" pragmatism.

---

[19] For a good ecclesiological explanation of the diverse nature of the local church—its biblical roots, theological significance, and practical outworkings—see Bruce Milne, *Dynamic Diversity: Bridging Class, Age, Race and Gender in the Church* (Downers Grove, IL: IVP, 2006).

[20] However, it must be noted with amazement that this elderly radio preacher has announced that the church age has been succeeded by the "radio age." See J. Ligon Duncan and Mark Talbot, *Should We Leave Our Churches? A Biblical Response to Harold Camping* (Phillipsburg: P&R, 2004).

Evangelism begins to resemble marketing, and church membership begins to resemble consumerism.[21]

Sacramentalist answer: high-church alternative services, the emerging church, "the Great Tradition." Still others believe the problem in the churches stem from a wrong (or at least unnecessary) focus on the subjective appropriation of the Christian faith by individuals. In response they advocate refocusing on the objective ordinances, or sacraments, of the church, not on individual responses of piety. Such sacramentalist responses can be found in great variety. Some multiservice congregations are offering alternative high-church services. Some in the "emerging church" movement are reengaging with pre-Reformation (and in some cases pre-Christian) practices of spirituality without fully comprehending the pre-Reformation understanding of the gospel often latent in such practices.

Among the Reformed, some are calling for an objectivism in the Christian life and profession which seems to deny any role for personal piety and subjective response to the gospel. Instead they are promoting a "federal vision" built specifically in opposition to what they regard as problematic evangelical pietism.[22] More generally many Protestant evangelicals are increasingly rejecting whatever is specifically evangelical or Protestant and replacing such distinctives with "the Great Tradition."[23]

Biblical answer: The church created by God's Spirit through his Word in the shape of his church. To these and many other putative solutions to current problems in the

---

[21] For a fascinating account of the influence of business practices in churches, see John Hardin, "Retailing Religion: Business Promotionalism in American Christian Churches in the Twentieth Century" (Unpublished Ph.D. dissertation, University of Maryland, 2011).

[22] See Guy Prentiss Waters, *The Federal Vision and Covenant Theology* (Phillipsburg, NJ: P&R Publishing, 2006).

[23] Sadly too many of these advocates, though they understand themselves to be Protestants, are taking the Roman Catholic position in the Reformation-era debates about the apostolicity of certain practices and doctrines. Concern for the teachings of the church fathers is nothing new among evangelicals. It was prominent in the work of Martin Luther, John Calvin, Thomas Cranmer, John Jewel, and other Reformers across Europe. But today's disputants lack the Reformers' experience of having lived in a Roman Catholic church that was unchallenged by Scripture and loaded down with centuries' worth of doctrinal accretions, accretions which had not been sifted by apostolic teaching.

churches, recourse must be relentlessly taken to Scripture. A clear understanding of the gospel is foundational for any genuine renewal in evangelical churches. Solutions treated as normative but which are not found in Scripture must be rejected as latter-day tradition that lacks the authority of the apostles. Ecclesiology cannot be reduced either to evangelism or to self-enhancement. In the Christian church the reigning consumer must become the repenting sinner, and the Christ-ordained sacraments are better not received than being received without personal faith (see 1 Cor 11:30). God creates his church by his Spirit through his Word. All other answers to the lack of discipleship in too many of today's churches compound the problems they intend to address.

This Matters for the Church's Character

The culture of the church, like the life of an individual, simply reflects the church's character. If the doctrine of the church enunciated in this chapter is to be applied, the practice of corrective church discipline must be recovered.

How to Practice Church Discipline Today

The recovery of church discipline requires viewing it as a natural part of church membership. It should be taught in new members classes. It should be addressed in sermons, testimonies, and newsletters. And books on the topic can be recommended. Too many people treat this topic apologetically and act as if admitting to the practice of discipline is regrettable. While the sins and their tragic consequences requiring discipline are of course regrettable, the attempt to correctively discipline unrepentant sin is not. When done in humility, prayer, and love, it edifies the body and glorifies God.[24]

One caution is in order here. Church discipline will seem odd and even offensive if introduced into a congregation not marked by a culture of mutual care, a desire to be

---

[24] For good practical instructions on carrying out church discipline, see Jay Adams, *Handbook of Church Discipline* (Grand Rapids: Ministry Resources Library, 1986); and Mark Dever, in *Polity: Biblical Arguments on How to Conduct Church Life* (Washington, DC: Center for Church Reform, 2001).

involved in one another's lives, and a passion for discipling in the faith. A pastor may desire to be obedient to Scripture, but congregations will feel that the deep involvement in their lives required by the practice of discipline is unnatural and wrong if things like church covenants and membership expectations have not been clearly taught. The first step toward practicing church discipline in a congregation is simply teaching the people to pray and care for one another. Learning to love and disciple one another—truly practicing the priesthood of all believers—is a prerequisite to introducing corrective discipline. Formative discipline must precede corrective discipline.

Why Practice Church Discipline Today?

Church discipline provides one part of the necessary response to the nominalism prevalent in churches today. Pastors must consider that following biblical instructions in every area of church life—including their practices of membership admission and discipline—may be the key to health lacking in their church. If pastors desire sinners to repent, they must realize that discipline is a biblical way to pursue that. If church leaders want their congregations to be characterized by thankfulness of heart and holiness of life, they should reexamine their practice of church discipline. The health of the whole church would be radically improved in many congregations by excommunicating those members who are committed to sins like nonattendance, divisiveness, adultery, or fornication more than they are committed to God's glory. The action of excluding the unrepentant enables the church to give a clear witness of the gospel to the world. And it ultimately brings glory to God, as his people more and more display his character of holy love.

This Matters for God's Glory

The Church as Display Evangelism

John L. Dagg concluded his introduction to his *Treatise on Church Order* with this appropriate admonition:

> Church order and the ceremonials of religion, are
> less important than a new heart; and in the view
> of some, any laborious investigation of questions
> respecting them may appear to be needless and
> unprofitable. But we know, from the Holy Scriptures,
> that Christ gave commands on these subjects, and we
> cannot refuse to obey. Love prompts our obedience;
> and love prompts also the search which may be nec-
> essary to ascertain his will. Let us, therefore, pros-
> ecute the investigations which are before us, with a
> fervent prayer, that the Holy Spirit, who guides into
> all truth, may assist us to learn the will of him whom
> we supremely love and adore.[25]

Many Protestants have begun to think that because
the church is not essential to the gospel, it is not important to the gospel. This is an unbiblical, false, and dangerous conclusion. Our churches are the proof of the gospel. In
the gatherings of the church, the Christian Scriptures are
read. In the ordinances of the church, the work of Christ
is depicted. In the life of the church, the character of God
himself should be evident. A church seriously compromised
in character would seem to make the gospel itself irrelevant.

The doctrine of the church is important because it is tied
to the good news itself. The church is to be the appearance of
the gospel. It is what the gospel looks like when played out
in people's lives. Take away the church and you take away the
visible manifestation of the gospel in the world. Christians in
churches, then, are called to practice "display evangelism,"
and the world will witness the reign of God begun in a community of people made in his image and reborn by his Spirit.
Christians, not just as individuals but as God's people bound
together in churches, are the clearest picture the world sees
of who God is and what his will is for them. Jesus said, "By
this all men will know that you are my disciples, if you love
one another" (John 13:35). And Paul stated, "His intent was
that now, through the church, the manifold wisdom of God
should be made known to the rulers and authorities in the

---

[25] Dagg, *Treatist on Church Order*, 12.

heavenly realms, according to his eternal purpose which he accomplished in Christ Jesus our Lord" (Eph 3:10–11).

Name Index

Subject Index

Scripture Index